"Joseph Nicholas dispels the misconcepti.. .... vesting is risk neutral in a compendious and well-written text. **This book is useful to both the practitioner and investor alike, providing insight into the mechanics, benefits, and risks of these valuable, diversifying strategies.**"

> —**Daniel Knight, CFA, Director, Portfolio Management**
> **Columbine Asset Management**

"**Joseph Nicholas has utilized his years at the center of the hedge fund industry to create a comprehensive road map to market-neutral investing.** The book provides an understandable analysis of the techniques, risks, and opportunities within this sometimes arcane corner of the investment world, tempered with the important distinction between market neutral and risk free."

> —**Gene T. Pretti, President & Chief Investment Officer**
> **Zazove Associates, LLC**

"**Joseph Nicholas has done a tremendous job of explaining the intricacies of and opportunities presented by the use of arbitrage and market-neutral strategies to achieve investment return and risk objectives.** These strategies represent the immediate future of investment management and investing. **This book is a must-read for all serious investment managers and investors!**"

> —**Greg Williamson, President**
> **Springfield Asset Management, L.L.C.**

"Joseph Nicholas has done an amazing job describing in detail a variety of arbitrage transactions. **This book goes a long way toward educating investors about what is really involved in these alternative investment strategies.**"

> —**Barry Newburger, Senior Managing Director**
> **Avery Capital Management**

Advance praise for
Market-Neutral Investing:
Long/Short Hedge Fund Strategies

"Market-neutral investing has come of age and is the fastest growing segment within the global hedge funds industry. Nicholas offers some unique and valuable insights into eight specific market-neutral strategies that are in growing demand by both institutional and private investors. **He provides a modular, pragmatic, and refreshing analysis of the specific attributes underpinning each investment strategy, related risks, and issues. This is a milestone publication, which broadens our knowledge and investment horizons—an invaluable reference tool for global portfolio managers, the international investment community, and industry service providers.**"

> **—Sohail Jaffer, Chairman**
> **Alternative Investment Management Association (AIMA)**

"**Joe has authored a text that all potential and current hedge fund investors should read.** This publication is sorely needed by the investment community and will help to broaden the number of investors participating in hedge funds."

> **—Jack Barry, President**
> **Beacon Hill Asset Management, LLC**

"**Sound, practical advice from one of the leading researchers in the hedge fund industry.** High net worth investors, institutional investors, and their advisors would be well advised to develop a working knowledge of the topics in this book. When it comes to finance and investing, hedge funds are the leading-edge technology."

> **—Vernon C. Sumnicht, MBA, CFP, President**
> **Sumnicht & Associates and Sumnicht Hedge Fund Advisors, LLC**

Market-Neutral Investing

Also available from
Bloomberg Press

Mastering Microcaps:
Strategies, Trends, and Stock Selection
by Daniel P. Coker

Risk:
The New Management Imperative in Finance
by James T. Gleason

Investing in Hedge Funds:
Strategies for the New Marketplace
by Joseph G. Nicholas

Small-Cap Dynamics:
Insights, Analysis, and Models
by Satya Dev Pradhuman

A complete list of our titles is available at
www.bloomberg.com/books

Attention Corporations

Bloomberg Press Books are available at quantity discounts with bulk purchase for sales promotional use and for corporate education or other business uses. Special editions or book excerpts can also be created. For information, please call 609-279-4670 or write to: Special Sales Dept., Bloomberg Press, P.O. Box 888, Princeton, NJ 08542.

Bloomberg Professional Library

Market-Neutral Investing

Long/Short Hedge Fund Strategies

JOSEPH G. NICHOLAS

Bloomberg Press
Princeton

Library of Congress Cataloging-in-Publication Data

Nicholas, Joseph G.
    Market-neutral investing : long/short hedge fund srategies /
Joseph G. Nicholas.
        p. cm. — (Bloomberg professional library)
    Includes index.
    ISBN 1-57660-037-8 (alk. paper)
    1. Hedge funds—United States.   2. Investment analysis.   I. Title.
II. Series.
    HG4930.N535 2000
    332.64'5—dc21

                                                        00-037952

Edited by Kathleen Peterson

First edition published 2000

1 3 5 7 9 10 8 6 4 2

To George, Frankie, Johnny, Julia,
Alexandra, Eric, Isabella, and Nicholas

Contents

8   Equity Hedge   177

9   Equity Market-Neutral and Statistical Arbitrage   203

Acknowledgments

I THANK THE FOLLOWING:

For his detailed strategy research and work on all aspects of the book: Ben Borton.

For their help in drawing out the details of the strategies: John Pagli, John Zerwick, John Calamos, Basil Williams, Tim Palmer, John Carlson, Jack Barry, Massoud Heidari, Barry Newberger, Peter Drippe, Marcus Jundt, Roger Richter, and Dan Knight.

For their insightful reading of the manuscript: George Benson, Brenna Berman, Robert M. Pine, and Peter Swank.

For her advice and ongoing assistance in developing the consulting business on which the insights in this book are founded: Lori Runquist.

For their work on the systemic risk-reducing aspects of market-neutral investing: Jianming Mao and Paul Alegnani.

For their help in building and improving the Hedge Fund Research database: all present and former employees of Hedge Fund Research.

For their stylistic and editorial recommendations: Kathleen Peterson and the staff at Bloomberg Press.

Foreword

For those of us who invest, the next step beyond constructing a basic, well-optimized portfolio of stocks and bonds is the introduction of diversifiers such as venture capital, private equity, natural resources, real estate and alternative strategies, of which hedge- and market-neutral investing are a part.

Market-neutral investments are attractive because they can substantially improve the performance characteristics of a traditional portfolio. A good market-neutral manager can produce better risk-adjusted returns than the market. Much of this is linked to the manager being able to take both long and short positions, perhaps using leverage as well. There is the dexterity that a manager can employ in exploiting niche inefficiencies. And there is the combination of experience and talent, which—though intangible—makes up are a large part of a successful manager's profile.

Market-neutral investing is not a panacea, however. It is too easily misinterpreted as risk-neutral, which it is not. It is immune neither to the influence of the market nor to the human fallibility to which all managers are subject. There are no perfectly hedged investments, and there will be variability when a market-neutral manager's performance is compared to his or her benchmark. The expectation should be for variability that is less extreme than that of conventional investments. Designing portfolios to include multiple managers who pursue separate substrategies within the same discipline can further smooth out this variability.

The maxim of investing only in that which you understand applies especially to market-neutral strategies. The complexities created by the combination of longs, shorts, and leverage make these strategies different from conventional investments—something akin to moving from a two-dimensional environment to three dimensions. There are many ways to use these basic elements, yielding a broad spectrum of possible results, from cautiously defensive to purely speculative. As well, it is important to know how managers get results using these tools. Some strategies depend just as much—or even more—on a manager's knack for scoping out inefficiencies and special opportunities.

Market-neutral strategies are understandable. The best approach to getting to know how one of these strategies works is first to break it down into its basic components, and then to examine how those parts interact as a system with its own specific behavior characteristics. That also happens to be how this book is organized. Once these fundamentals have been taken care of, you can be confident in evaluating a strategy's place in your portfolio, moving ahead with identification and selection of managers, and judging the effectiveness of your market-neutral investing.

Joe Nicholas and I have collaborated over the last several years in developing and fine-tuning the alternative investment portfolio for the Michigan State University Foundation. Working with Joe has expanded my perspective on investing and I am pleased that he has condensed so much of his encyclopedic knowledge into the pages of this book.

His discussion of the subject is especially timely, considering the growing recognition of market-neutral investments as a component of diversification. Investors, consultants, and investment professionals should find it invaluable in deepening their understanding of the field.

GEORGE BENSON
Executive Director
Michigan State University Foundation

Introduction

A s I completed my earlier book, *Investing in Hedge Funds: Strategies for the New Marketplace,* in the fall of 1998, an increasing number of questions about market-neutral investing began to flow into the offices of Hedge Fund Research (HFR). These inquiries were motivated by events such as the failure of Long Term Capital Management and the over and underperformance of market-neutral funds in 1998. Some of the funds in question performed quite well during the period, and others were less successful; yet both types were promoted as "market neutral."

In today's volatile markets, it is not hard to see the allure of the market-neutral tag. Investors have expressed a compelling need to protect some portion of their assets by making allocations to strategies that provide a hedge to equity exposure but yield higher returns than bonds. Astute marketers have offered them market-neutral products as a solution. However, it would be dangerous and incorrect to assume that strategies described as market neutral are without risks. The purpose of this book is to flush out what is really meant by "market neutral" and to describe the possible benefits and risks associated with investments in market-neutral strategies.

Volatile markets, such as those experienced in recent years, are eye-openers for investors. Many investors who made market-neutral investments during this period could not describe what the term actually means. Nor were they fully aware of the risk and reward characteristics of the funds or strategies they had (or wished to be) invested in. Many did not realize that the term "market neutral" is used to describe not one, but a variety of distinct investment strategies and approaches. To many investors, "market neutral" sounds like "risk free" and, accordingly, it is used effectively by marketers to that end. But because an investment strategy has characteristics that allow it to be classified as market neutral does not mean that it is without risk. And the risk of the different strategies that can be called market neutral varies substantially.

This book was undertaken to provide some answers to these questions and to describe, in detail, the various market-neutral approaches. The questions were prompted by specific events, but many of the answers are timeless and touch on the essentials of investing and risk management. I have drawn extensively on HFR's database of over 3,000 hedge funds and on the daily portfolio analysis that we conduct for many of our hedge fund portfolios. I also have incorporated extensive input and actual investment examples provided by managers and practitioners of each of the strategies.

Chapter 1 lays out the general concepts of market-neutral investing: long and short positions, the use of leverage, and arbitrage. From these basic concepts, I proceed to the concept that links market-neutral strategies: relationship investing. Unlike traditional, directional long or short selling strategies, this form of investing derives returns from changes in the price relationship between two related instruments. This is not to say that market-neutral strategies do not contain directional exposures as well; however, the nature of these exposures, and the associated risks, differ fundamentally from traditional strategies.

Chapter 2 introduces the largest practitioners of market-neutral strategies: hedge fund managers, growth trends and size of the hedge fund industry, and performance of market-neutral strategies over the past ten years.

Chapter 3 explores investing using market-neutral strategies. It addresses concepts such as modern portfolio theory; incorporating market-neutral strategies in an investment portfolio; transparency; and risk management. Finally, it introduces the strategies most commonly described as market neutral.

Each of the remaining chapters covers one of the market-neutral strategies. Chapter 9 covers equity hedge, also known as long/short equity. This strategy is not considered market neutral because it may be operated with a long or short (usually long) directional bias. It has been included as a point of comparison and because many of the principles of relationship investing apply to the strategy.

The afterword examines the future of market-neutral investing and recaps the approach to understanding this investment niche laid out in this book.

Investing in Relationships

1

WHAT IS MARKET NEUTRAL?

"**M**arket-neutral" investing refers to a group of investment strategies that seek to neutralize certain market risks by taking offsetting long and short positions in instruments with actual or theoretical relationships. These approaches seek to limit exposure to systemic changes in price caused by shifts in macro-economic variables or market sentiment.

The market-neutral and hedged strategies discussed in this book are: convertible arbitrage, fixed-income arbitrage, mortgage-backed securities arbitrage, merger arbitrage, equity market neutral, statistical arbitrage, relative value arbitrage, and equity hedge. These strategies invest in very different asset types, ranging from equities to Treasury bonds to options to mortgage-backed securities. Thus, if we look at these strategies in a conventional manner—by asset type—they bear little resemblance to one another.

Convertible arbitrageurs take long positions in convertible securities and short positions in common stocks. Fixed-income arbitrageurs take long and short positions in different kinds of fixed-income instruments. Merger arbitrageurs take long and short positions in the stocks of companies involved in mergers. Yet all of these strategies are described as market neutral. How can these apparently disparate investment strategies fall into one grouping? *Market-neutral strategies all derive returns from the relationship between a long and a short component of the portfolio, whether that relationship takes place at the level of individual instruments or at the portfolio level.*

By taking long and short positions in amounts that neutralize market risks, market-neutral strategies trade exposure to the *market* for exposure to the *relationship* between the long and short sides of their portfolios. As we shall see, these relationships are not *a priori* less volatile than the directional fortunes of the market, although they have proved in recent history to be more stable than the traditional market measures. Market-neutral investing should not replace investments in traditional asset classes; rather, they complement traditional investments in fixed income and equities because they represent an alternative and uncorrelated source of return. Thus, market neutral *does not* imply risk-free investing. It *does* mean taking on risks that are different from those associated with the directional caprices of traditional long-only investments in asset classes. By adding a different and uncorrelated source of return to a traditional portfolio of stocks and bonds, investors can diversify their overall risk and improve the risk and reward characteristics of their investments.

As illustrated in Figure 1.1, the performance characteristics for these approaches have been attractive during the past decade. The risk to return profiles of market-neutral strategies outperformed long-only strategies. Almost all of the market-neutral indexes reside above a straight line drawn from the risk-free rate

Figure 1.1   Hedge Fund Strategies: Risk to Return Profiles,
January 1990–December 1999*

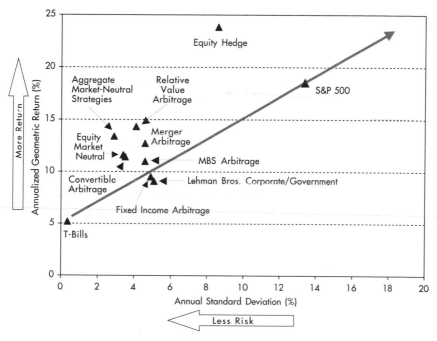

* *Note:* MBS Arbitrage data only available for January 1993–December 1999.

offered by Treasury bills through the profile for the S&P 500 (the most widely accepted proxy for the stock market).

However, one must be careful regarding the conclusions drawn from this observation. The third quarter of 1998 reminded the financial world that past results are not necessarily indicative of future results. With that warning in place, we can safely make a number of important observations.

1. Any investment strategy that consistently confounds the accepted relationship between risk and reward is taking advantage of a

pocket of inefficiency in the market. Investors who utilize these strategies have a competitive advantage that allows them to exploit that inefficiency. For many practitioners of market-neutral strategies, that advantage is simply the ability to sell securities short. This simple constraint precludes most mutual funds and other traditional long-only investment vehicles from using market-neutral strategies. The foremost practitioners of market-neutral strategies are the proprietary desks of major financial institutions and hedge fund managers who are not subject to the same regulations as mutual fund managers.

2. Market-neutral investment strategies require practitioners to invest in information technology and infrastructure. Historically, this fixed cost has represented another barrier to entry into these investment approaches. However, advances in information technologies and the reductions in the cost of these technologies during the 1990s leveled the financial playing field and opened up these strategies to a new generation of boutique money-management firms. The ideas underlying market-neutral investment strategies have been circulating for at least a half-century, but practical implementation of these strategies has only recently become possible for small firms.

3. Investment strategies that provide stable risk-adjusted returns will, over time, attract both investor funds and new practitioners. It is often difficult to determine the extent to which the proprietary desks of major financial institutions are involved in such activities, but there is ample evidence of growing interest (and assets) in market-neutral strategies among hedge funds. With more managers and capital relying on the relationships between securities that are major sources of market-neutral returns, some of these relative pricing inefficiencies will be reduced or will disappear. This risk—the repeatability of returns—will be touched on in each of the specific strategy chapters in this book. It is important to note that although some of the returns from inefficient

pricing will be wiped out, the structural features of the financial world will always produce pockets of pricing inefficiency between related securities. Market-neutral strategies are positioned to take advantage of current and future pricing inefficiencies.

4. The preliminary results of research being conducted by Hedge Fund Research (HFR) indicate that single practitioners of market-neutral strategies may outperform an index of managers utilizing the same strategy during any given period, but it is unlikely that the same practitioner will continue to outperform the index in the next period of the same length. Similarly, two managers pursuing the same substrategy on a diversified basis cannot significantly outperform an index of such managers. These observations are in line with academic research indicating that actively managed equity portfolios will rarely outperform an index of stocks over time.

Just as a core return can be said to be attributable to an asset class such as equities, a core return is attributable to each market-neutral strategy. Investors would therefore be well advised to spend more time understanding the underlying strategies and less time trying to pick the best manager. This observation has led some investors to seek out indexes for these strategies and to explore the idea of making the strategies investable. This would isolate the core return attributable to the strategy and would dampen the volatility that may be associated with any given manager in the index.

5. As market-neutral strategies, to a greater or lesser extent, derive returns from relationships between securities rather than from the direction of an asset class, they can be said to have a different source of return than traditional investments. These strategies are only now reaching maturity. As a group, they have clearly outperformed traditional asset classes on a risk-adjusted basis during the past decade. In and of itself, this observation does not tell us what to expect in the future, but it provides an impetus to search for an explanation for the past results and to formulate

expectations for the future. The first step is to try to understand the strategies themselves. That is the purpose of this book.

BASIC CONCEPTS

As with any specialized investment niche, there are certain concepts that are essential to understanding market-neutral strategies such as, hedging, leverage, short selling, markets, exposures, derivatives, and arbitrage. To avoid confusion, important investment concepts that recur throughout the book are defined below. For experienced investors, these explanations may seem elementary, but it is important to establish their meanings in the present context. (A complete glossary precedes the index; see page 249.)

position: A particular holding within a portfolio (for example, 1,000 shares of Citigroup).

market: A place where buyers and sellers of securities make exchanges. Historically, markets have been tangible places such as the New York Stock Exchange or the Chicago Board of Options Exchange, but the advent of networked computers has transferred much of the "action" to cyberspace.

exposure: The amount of risk a position faces in the market. Because particular markets contain risks, taking a position in one of those markets "exposes" the investor to that market's risks. For example, investors might have exposure not only to equities, fixed income, or currency, but also to subsets, such as market sectors.

directional exposure: The amount of risk an *unhedged* position faces in the market as compared to the net exposure of positions involving long and short hedged relationships.

hedging: Any investment that is taken in conjunction with another position in order to reduce directional exposure. A classic example is farmers who enter into futures contracts for grain, to lock in a particular price. They remove any uncertainty about the price they will receive for the grain, but they forgo the possibility of receiving a higher price.

short selling: Borrowing a security and selling it on the open market, and buying it back later (ideally, at a lower price). The intention is to benefit from a decrease in the price of the security. Short positions can be taken as hedges for an associated long position, or as stand-alone investments.

derivatives: A derivative is any financial instrument for which the value is directly dependent on the price of another asset. Good examples include options (the price of a stock option depends on the price of the underlying stock) and futures contracts (the price of a futures contract depends on the price of the underlying asset).

leverage: The use of borrowed funds or of derivatives to create exposures that are in excess of the amount of investable assets. For example, leverage can be used to create an exposure of one and a half dollars for every dollar invested.

liquidity: The ability of an investor to sell an asset in a timely fashion. When there are few buyers for a particular asset, that asset is said to be illiquid.

pure arbitrage: The simultaneous purchase and sale of the same instruments at different prices when the risk to profit is zero. For example, if you buy gold for $100 on one side of the street, walk across the street, and sell it for $110 on the other side, you are making a 10 percent "sure" profit on the simultaneous buy and sell.

relative value arbitrage: The simultaneous purchase and sale of related instruments, wherein the profit on such a trade depends on a favorable change in the relationship between the prices of the instruments.

correlation: A term from regression analysis that describes the strength of the relationship between a dependent and an independent variable. Assets, or strategies, are correlated if the returns they provide are similar to one another in similar market environments.

Relationship Investing

Many definitions are given for *market-neutral investing*. In general, as noted at the beginning of this chapter, the term indicates an approach to investing that includes constructing a portfolio with offsetting long and short exposures in one or more markets. Some aspect of market exposure is neutralized through short selling or otherwise obtaining an offsetting exposure to a long position. This may be done in a general sense—for example, by hedging interest rates—or in a subset, such as neutralizing exposure to stocks in a market sector such as technology. The most common technique is to take a short position in an instrument closely related to a long exposure, thus hedging out exposure to "market risks" that affect both securities equally. Market-neutral strategies are intended to "neutralize" these systemic market risks through offsetting long and short positions.

This book discusses a number of strategies that can be called market neutral. The list is by no means exhaustive, but some of the larger, better known approaches are analyzed. Although these strategies sometimes involve disparate investment approaches, all of them seek to derive returns from the relationship between the values of two or more securities.

Relationship investing involves a nondirectional approach. The return to the strategy comes from the net result of the long and short components (the performance of the long position relative to the short position). However, the return does not always come solely from a nondirectional exposure. In some cases, the former assessment is accurate; returns are generated from changes in value of matched long and short positions (such as in explicit pairs trading). But, in many other cases, the short component hedges, or neutralizes, part of the long exposure, leaving an unhedged, residual directional exposure. When such a position is leveraged, the result is a leveraged directional exposure. Market-neutral approaches do not eliminate risk entirely; rather, they allow managers to hedge unwanted risks and retain exposure to risks they wish to maintain.

UNDERSTANDING MARKET-NEUTRAL APPROACHES

The key to understanding market-neutral approaches is to identify the different long and short exposures, and to determine which of them are hedge relationships, or which are unhedged, directional, exposures outside the hedge—or a combination of both.

For example, consider two hypothetical equities: A and B. Suppose that A and B experience the same fluctuations in value due to a change in interest rate policy. They differ, however, in that A has a significantly stronger earnings forecast. A traditional, long-only manager would take a position in A, forget about B, and derive the returns solely from the fortunes of A (which are driven by both the characteristics A shares with B, and the characteristics unique to A).

A market-neutral manager, on the other hand, would take a long position in A but would offset that position with an equal short position in B. In doing so, the manager eliminates the exposure to the shared characteristics of the two instruments and derives returns solely from the relative performance of A and B. Instrument A could actually drop in value and the manager would still turn a profit so long as B dropped more. Unfortunately, the relationships between two securities are rarely this simple. The next example shows how the relationship between two securities becomes more complex as more securities are added.

Consider three instruments: A, B, and C. As in the preceding example, instrument A shares characteristics with instrument B, but also shares characteristics with C. Suppose that 50 percent of A's characteristics are shared with B, which we will represent as A(B), and 50 percent are shared with C, represented as A(C). The investment position is long 100 A and short 50 B. The long exposure to A equates to a long exposure to A(B) and A(C). The return comes from a change in the relationship between A and B: the net in price change of A and of B. But one must delve further. What drives the price movements of the different instruments?

A closer look reveals the actual exposures and source of return. The short exposure to B neutralizes the long exposure to A(B), so long as A(B) is highly correlated to A, leaving a directional long exposure to A(C). The source of return can come from:

1. A change in the relationship between A(B) and B.
2. A change in the value of the directional component A(C).
3. A combination of both.

Table 1.1 depicts the underlying exposures of the position and the various sources of return from Period 1 to Period 2 to Period 3. This example begins with a long position of 100 A and a short

Table 1.1 Comparative Exposures and Sources of Return

Exposures	Beginning Position Values	Period 1	Period 2	Period 3
100 A	**195**	**200**	**184**	**212**
(50) B	**(100)**	**(100)**	**(90)**	**(110)**
0 C	100	100	90	102
A(B)	95	100	94	114
A(C)	100	100	90	98
Gain (Loss)		**5**	**(6)**	**8**

position of 50 B. Initially, A is the equivalent of 50 B and 50 C. When the positions are initiated, A is valued at 195 and B at 100. The value of A can be broken down into two components: A(C) valued at 100, and A(B) valued at 95. Fifty shares of B are sold short, to offset the exposure to A(B). As we shall see, this short position may represent a perfect or imperfect hedge, depending on the correlation (strength of the relationship) between the value of B and A(B). The residual exposure to A(C) is a directional exposure.

In Period 1, the net change in the relationship between the A and B exposures was 5 (the appreciation of A from 195 to 200). The value of B did not change. The change in the value of A was due to an appreciation in the value of the A(B) component from 95 to 100. The A(C) component did not change in value. In this case, the relationship between B and A(B) is imperfect. The characteristics that are shared by B and A(B) caused the value of A(B) to increase. Other factors influenced the price of B, and its value remained unchanged. The hedge was imperfect and reflected the manager's opinion of relative valuations rather than a hedge against an explicit risk. A manager might construct such a hedge if he or she believed that instrument A was cheap or mispriced relative to instrument B, due to structural events in the market or supply-and-demand constraints. Suppose that the manager felt that, because of a market distortion, A ought to be valued at 200 and B was correctly valued at 100. In this case, the relationship between A(B) and B is not correctly reflected in the relative valuations of A and B. The positive return in the period is derived from the change in the relationship between A(B) and B.

In Period 2, the change in the value relationship between A and B was negative 6. A depreciated by 16, and the short B exposure lost 10. But while B depreciated by 10, from 100 to 90, A(B) depreciated by 12, resulting in a loss of 2 on the hedge. The hedge was imperfect, but it significantly dampened the loss on the long position in A. At the same time, A(C) depreciated by 4. Thus, the net loss on the whole position was 6. In this case, a loss on an imperfect hedge has resulted, and it is not compensated for by a gain in the directional component.

In Period 3, the change in the value relationship between A and B is positive 8. In this scenario, B and A(B) moved in 100 percent correlation. A(B) declined in value by 10, but the short B exposure perfectly hedged, or neutralized, the exposure to A(B), generating an increase in value of 10 to offset A(B)'s loss. The overall position gain was due entirely to an increase in the value of A(C), the unhedged, directional exposure in the position. This is an example of how a market-neutral manager would go about neutralizing a particular risk in favor of another, more favorable risk.

To understand how leverage affects risk exposures in a market-neutral position, one needs to understand the relationship of the long position to the short position. Leverage multiplies the risk associated with residual directional exposures. Theoretically, the risk to perfectly hedged components is not increased by applying leverage. However, as demonstrated in the preceding example, with only three securities, perfect hedges are not always available, nor are they always desirable. Imagine how much harder they are to construct at the portfolio level, when a manager has a universe of thousands of instruments from which to choose.

The examples presented here show how market-neutral managers analyze possible investments in a general sense. How these general concepts play out in specific strategies and markets is shown in Chapters 4 through 11. For now, it is enough to emphasize that market-neutral positions must be broken down into the different component exposures, and the relationships must be evaluated to determine how well undesirable exposures can be hedged. If an asset offers both a desirable exposure and an undesirable exposure that can be perfectly hedged, then the manager will hedge against the undesirable exposure and isolate the desirable exposure. If such undesirable exposures cannot be perfectly hedged, the probability of profit from the residual directional exposure must outweigh the probability of a loss on the hedge. Alternatively, a manager could initiate a position based purely on a discrepancy in relative valuations, and wait for the values to converge.

Chapter 2 presents developments in the hedge fund industry. Chapter 3 provides essential guidelines and reasons for investing in market-neutral strategies and introduces each of the core strategies. Later chapters have detailed discussions of individual strategies.

Developments in the Hedge Fund Industry

2

The largest practitioners of market-neutral investment strategies are the proprietary trading desks of major financial institutions and hedge fund managers. Because of the difficulty in ascertaining the extent of proprietary involvement, the discussion here focuses on hedge fund managers who utilize market-neutral strategies. This little known group of money managers have adopted a wide variety of specialized investment strategies and constitute one of the fastest growing and exciting areas of the investment world.

The high-profile failure and subsequent bailout of Long Term Capital Management (LTCM) gave many market participants, politicians, and investors their introduction to or their first consideration of hedge funds. One of the unfortunate side effects of this negative introduction to the private investment industry is that, in the minds of many, all hedge funds have been lumped together into one group. The behavior of a single firm should not be taken as indicative of an entire industry. All hedge funds are not alike, and there is much to be gained by judging each by its underlying investment strategy rather than dismissing them all because of the actions of one large anomalous firm. This book is designed to emphasize the underlying investment strategies rather than individual managers.

HEDGE FUND INDUSTRY ASSETS

From January 1990 to December 1999, the hedge fund industry's assets increased dramatically, from $20 billion to nearly $500 billion. Over the same period, the number of hedge funds increased from 200 to an estimated 3,500. This general growth masks changes in the composition of the underlying strategies utilized by hedge fund managers. Prior to 1990, the hedge fund sector was somewhat fragmented and was dominated by a small number of large global macro managers who made large, leveraged, speculative bets on macroeconomic events. The hedge fund sector is now more diverse and mature. Fueled by the longest bull market in history, and by rapid technological gains that have made information about these private investment vehicles more available, investors have become more comfortable about allocating capital into hedge funds that offer sources of return and risk profiles that differ from those of traditional stock and bond portfolios. Figure 2.1 shows the growth of hedge fund assets in the 1990s.

A great number of factors have contributed to the rapid growth of both hedge funds and hedge fund assets. Among the most important factors are:

1. *Alternative sources of return.* Hedge funds, particularly those that utilize market-neutral strategies, provide return streams that have low correlation to traditional asset classes. Thus, they provide a ready source of diversification.

2. *Opportunity.* The continuing expansion of global markets and the ongoing development of new capital markets provide

Figure 2.1 Growth of Industry: Hedge Fund Asset Growth, January 1990–December 1999

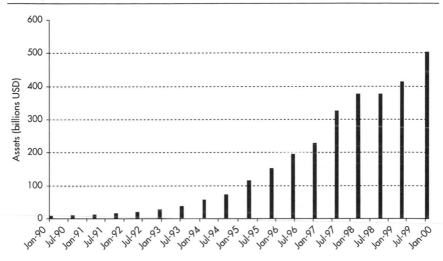

an expanding arena for astute investment managers who are able to exploit pricing inefficiencies.

3. *Tools and support services.* The explosion in investment technology has made more information available that is more accurate on a timely basis. At the same time, it allows market participants to analyze this information more quickly and thoroughly, at lower cost.

4. *Talent and expertise.* As a result of the reduced cost of technology and data, returns have become less dependent on large and costly infrastructure, and the value of talented individuals with a firm grasp of specialized investment strategies has increased. Investment funds naturally flow to money managers who offer knowledge, expertise, and talent.

5. *Favorable markets.* The 1990s bull market created an enormous amount of wealth. Against that backdrop, hedge fund managers have found it easier to raise capital.

6. _Performance_. Even with all the other factors, the industry would not have grown without producing results. With few exceptions, the investment strategies pursued by hedge fund managers have generated attractive risk-adjusted returns.

HEDGE FUND INVESTORS

Before 1990, hedge fund investors were composed almost entirely of high-net-worth individuals. But as more information has become available about the nature of hedge fund strategies and the risk-to-return profiles they offer, institutions have come to represent a larger part of the assets invested in hedge funds.

Today, the pool of U.S. investors is still dominated by high-net-worth individuals; they comprise 40 percent of the U.S. dollars invested in the hedge fund industry. However, as shown in Figure 2.2, there is a strong presence of other investors: U.S. pension

Figure 2.2 Estimated Percentage of Funds Invested by U.S. Investors in Hedge Funds

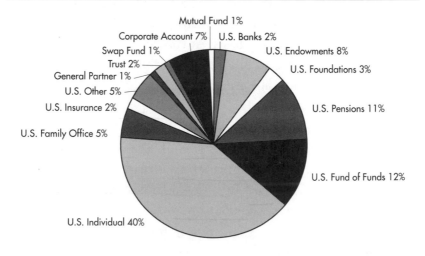

Mutual Fund 1%
Corporate Account 7% | U.S. Banks 2%
Swap Fund 1%
Trust 2%
General Partner 1%
U.S. Other 5%
U.S. Insurance 2%
U.S. Family Office 5%
U.S. Endowments 8%
U.S. Foundations 3%
U.S. Pensions 11%
U.S. Fund of Funds 12%
U.S. Individual 40%

Percentages have been rounded from data figures

funds, 11 percent; endowments, 8 percent; corporate accounts, 7 percent; family offices, 5 percent; foundations, 3 percent; insurance companies, 2 percent; and banks, 2 percent. Other investors represented at slightly lower levels include swap funds and mutual funds. An additional 12 percent comes from a fund of funds; however, it is difficult to identify the underlying investors in these funds. Anecdotal evidence indicates that many fund of funds investors are institutional.

Interestingly, foreign investment, with fewer regulations than U.S. investment, has become even more diversified, as illustrated in Figure 2.3. Individuals comprise only 17 percent of foreign investment in hedge funds. However, many foreign individuals channel their investments through foreign banks, which account for 23 percent of foreign investment. Pension funds and family offices make up 5 percent and 6 percent, respectively, of industry investment. Foreign insurance companies, corporate accounts, and foundations have also begun to invest in hedge funds.

Figure 2.3 Estimated Percentage of Hedge Funds Invested by Non–U.S. Investors

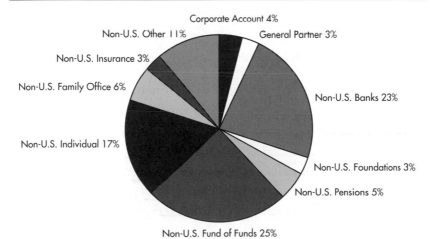

Corporate Account 4%

Non-U.S. Other 11%

General Partner 3%

Non-U.S. Insurance 3%

Non-U.S. Family Office 6%

Non-U.S. Banks 23%

Non-U.S. Individual 17%

Non-U.S. Foundations 3%

Non-U.S. Pensions 5%

Non-U.S. Fund of Funds 25%

Percentages have been rounded from data figures

The level of investor diversification varies by strategy. Many of the market-neutral strategies, such as convertible arbitrage and equity market neutral, have significant investments from many institutional sources.

Endowments, foundations, pension plans, family offices, banks, insurance companies, and other corporate entities have all made allocations to hedge funds with the goal of diversifying their source of return and reducing their portfolio risk. A good example of a European institution that has allocated funds to alternative investments is Nestlé's $4.1 billion Swiss Pension Fund. *Pensions and Investments* magazine estimates that the fund is in the top decile of Swiss pension funds in terms of returns. Fifty percent of the fund is invested in equities (two-fifths of which is indexed), and 29 percent is invested in fixed income, evenly split between European and foreign bonds. As of 1997, the fund had allocated 6 percent to hedge funds and other alternative investments. In fact, the Nestlé fund has set up a separate company, Unigestion Asset Management Guernsey, to select hedge-fund managers.[1] The purpose of the group is to identify managers who provide positive returns with low correlation with equities.

HEDGE FUND STRATEGIES

Like the term *mutual fund, hedge fund* does not refer to a specific investment approach or asset class. And while there is no formal definition, *hedge fund* generally describes a variety of alternative investment strategies that (1) utilize liquid and semiliquid instruments, and (2) are usually accessed by investing in private commingled funds. Most, but not all, make use of short-selling and hedging techniques, as well as various forms of leverage—although there are

---

[1] *Pension and Investments,* July 26, 1999, p. 61.

funds that are neither hedged nor leveraged. The key to understanding the industry is realizing that it consists of a diverse mix of sometimes unrelated investment strategies.

During the 1990s, rapid gains in technology leveled the financial playing field. As a result, many boutique money management operations utilizing market-neutral investment strategies emerged, and they changed the strategy composition within the hedge fund industry. Figures 2.4 and 2.5 show the composition of hedge fund strategies in 1990 and 1999, respectively.

Each of the market-neutral and hedged strategies covered in this book (equity market neutral, equity hedge, merger arbitrage, convertible arbitrage, relative value arbitrage, statistical arbitrage, mortgage-backed securities arbitrage, and fixed-income arbitrage) has made significant gains over the past decade. These strategies may be added to a traditional portfolio to enhance performance, to hedge against market declines, to provide diversification into other markets and instruments, or to introduce noncorrelating exposures.

ERic

Figure 2.4   Strategy Composition—1990

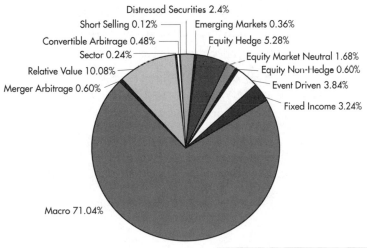

Distressed Securities 2.4%
Short Selling 0.12%
Emerging Markets 0.36%
Convertible Arbitrage 0.48%
Equity Hedge 5.28%
Sector 0.24%
Equity Market Neutral 1.68%
Relative Value 10.08%
Equity Non-Hedge 0.60%
Merger Arbitrage 0.60%
Event Driven 3.84%
Fixed Income 3.24%
Macro 71.04%

Percentages have been rounded from data figures

Figure 2.5 Strategy Composition—1999

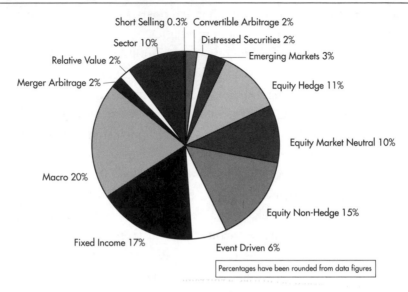

Short Selling 0.3% Convertible Arbitrage 2%
Sector 10% Distressed Securities 2%
Relative Value 2% Emerging Markets 3%
Merger Arbitrage 2% Equity Hedge 11%
Equity Market Neutral 10%
Macro 20% Equity Non-Hedge 15%
Fixed Income 17% Event Driven 6%

Percentages have been rounded from data figures

The strategies selected should meet the investor's objectives and constraints. Because most hedge fund managers pursue only one (or a related group) of approaches, investors should focus on the risk-and-reward characteristics of the strategies themselves.

The key to the industry is to understand the underlying strategies' risk-and-return characteristics and the market factors that affect them. In this, hedge funds are similar to other investment opportunities: analysis of returns is incomplete without an understanding of the potential risks. Chapter 3 gives evidence of why investors should consider an investment in market-neutral strategies, a brief introduction to the strategies covered at length later in this book, and some insights into how to go about accessing these strategies.

Making an Investment in Market-Neutral Strategies

3

Market-neutral strategies offer competitive returns with lower volatility than traditional long-only investments in equities and bonds. In addition, as a group they have low correlation to traditional investments in stocks and bonds. Both of these characteristics allow investors to improve risk-adjusted returns by diversifying a portion of a traditional portfolio of stocks and bonds into low-correlation market-neutral strategies.

This chapter provides evidence to support this claim, using linear analysis and mean variance optimization; introduces the core market-neutral strategies that are covered at length later in the book; and describes issues that investors should consider before making an allocation. These issues include matching investor objectives with investment opportunities, and reviewing the possible risks involved in accessing market-neutral strategies. The chapter also introduces a powerful new tool that prudent investors are using to alleviate many of those risks: daily transparency.

LINEAR ANALYSIS OF RETURNS

A common way of examining a stream of returns is by comparing the returns with those of a benchmark. The most common method is to compare them to a proxy for the overall stock market such as the S&P 500. Using traditional linear regression analysis we can determine the relationship between the returns generated by a strategy (the dependent variable) and the market return (the independent variable). The relationship is described by the regression line that is the best linear fit between the two streams of returns. The equation of the line takes the form $y = a + bx$, where y is the strategy return less the risk free interest rate, a is alpha (the y-intercept), b is beta (the slope of the line), and x is the market return less the risk free rate. The risk-free rate is subtracted from total return in order to represent the return that is attributable to the additional risk of a passive investment in the stock market, or an actively managed market-neutral strategy.

Three important indications are produced through linear regression analysis. First, the analysis produces a correlation statistic, referred to as r, which indicates the direction and strength of the relationship between the two streams of returns. Thus, a correlation of 1 would indicate that a 1 percent increase in the stock market return would be accompanied by a proportional increase in the strategy return. Second, beta indicates the magnitude of that relationship and is generally accepted as a proxy for systemic stock market risk. For example, a beta of 2.0 indicates that for a 1 percent increase in the stock market return we would expect the portion of the strategy return explained by market return (as indicated by the correlation statistic) to increase by 2 percent. Last, alpha indicates the residual portion of the strategy return that is unexplained by fluctuations in the stock market return. It is widely accepted as a measure of the value added through active portfolio management.

As indicated in Table 3.1, market-neutral strategies tend to have low correlation and low betas to the stock market. Thus, their returns are largely independent of stock market fluctuations. The portion of the return unexplained by stock market fluctuations, alpha, should be highlighted. Although alpha is commonly thought of as management skill, it should be emphasized that some portion is attributable to the strategy itself. Market-neutral strategies are designed to take advantage of pricing inefficiencies in financial markets, and as such, are alpha-oriented.

By adding market-neutral strategies to a traditional portfolio of stocks and bonds volatility, as measured by standard deviation, and systemic risk, as measured by beta, can be reduced without a corresponding reduction in returns. This pleasant paradox suggests that inefficiencies exist in financial markets, and that astute

Table 3.1   Statistical Profiles January 1990 to December 1999 (with Risk-Free Rate Subtracted)

Strategy	Average Monthly Rate of Return	Monthly Standard Deviation	Correlation to S&P 500	Beta to S&P 500	Alpha
S&P 500	0.8620	3.870	1	1	0
Convertible Arbitrage	0.5159	1.019	0.4027	0.401	0.425
Fixed Income Arbitrage	0.3609	1.429	−0.0956	−0.100	0.393
MBS Arbitrage (data only available 1/1993 to 12/1999)	0.4838	1.337	−0.0310	−0.040	0.499
Equity Hedge	1.4256	2.527	0.6453	0.645	1.063
Equity Market Neutral	0.5178	0.973	0.2548	0.253	0.463
Statistical Arbitrage	0.5273	1.088	0.4735	0.472	0.413
Merger Arbitrage	0.6054	1.339	0.5040	0.502	0.456
Relative Value Arbitrage	0.7213	1.191	0.3477	0.346	0.630

money managers armed with investment strategies designed to take advantage of these pricing inefficiencies may be able to produce higher risk-adjusted returns than the market. The excess return at each level of systemic risk is largely attributable to the alpha generated by each of the market-neutral strategies.

The riskiness of a portfolio as measured by variance of returns depends on the correlation among its holdings rather than the average variance of the separate components. Thus, adding an allocation that is highly correlated to an existing portfolio will not generally reduce the portfolio's overall volatility, because it will move in lockstep with the existing contents. On the other hand, adding a low correlation allocation, particularly one that exhibits low volatility as a stand-alone investment, can reduce overall portfolio volatility. The idea is to make allocations to strategies that will perform well in different market environments. Table 3.2 details the correlation of each of the market-neutral and hedged

Table 3.2 Correlation Matrix of Market-Neutral and Hedged Strategies, 1990–1999

1/1990 to 12/1999 *Correlation Matrix*	*Convert Arb*	*E. Hedge*	*Equity MN*	*FI Arb*
HFRI Convertible Arbitrage	1			
HFRI Equity Hedge Index	0.516	1		
HFRI Equity Market Neutral	0.183	0.466	1	
HFRI Fixed Income Arbitrage	0.124	0.036	0.067	1
HFRI Merger Arbitrage Index	0.482	0.473	0.149	−0.082
HFRI Relative Value Arbitrage Index	0.552	0.518	0.201	0.308
HFRI Statistical Arbitrage Index	0.187	0.252	0.577	0.096
HFRI Fixed Income: Mortgage-Backed Index*	0.360	0.138	0.234	0.658
Lehman Brothers Government/ Corporate Aggregate Index	0.230	0.137	0.184	−0.274
S&P 500 with Dividends	0.398	0.642	0.246	−0.100

* HFRI Fixed Income Mortgage-Backed Index data only available from 1993 to 1999.

strategies to the Lehman Brothers Government/Corporate Aggregate Fixed Income Index and the S&P 500, as well as to each other.

Note that the market-neutral strategies are not highly correlated with one another [except in cases such as fixed-income arbitrage and mortgage-backed securities (MBS) arbitrage, or convertible arbitrage and relative value arbitrage, where the two strategies overlap], or with the major stock and bond indexes. This indicates that a portfolio of market-neutral strategies will produce returns with less variance than traditional investments. Using mean variance optimization, it can be illustrated that adding an allocation to market-neutral strategies to a portfolio of stocks and bonds can reduce risk without a proportional decrease in returns.

We are now entering an era when mean variance optimization can be used as a tool to construct portfolios of market-neutral hedge funds. In the past, such analysis was difficult because of a

Merger Arb	RVA	Stat Arb	MBS Arb	Bonds	Stocks
1					
0.392	1				
0.244	0.200	1			
0.089	0.331	0.116	1		
0.114	0.042	0.427	0.111	1	
0.499	0.345	0.483	−0.033	0.395	1

lack of data (historical data were sparse and unreliable at best, prior to 1990). The hedge fund industry is private, and managers have no obligation to make performance information public. However, in response to investor demand, particularly from institutions, a large number of hedge funds now make performance results available to various database groups. With a decade's worth of performance data now available, it is possible to make a retrospective analysis of optimal asset allocations based on mean variance optimization, and to begin to build expectations for optimal allocations in the future.

Mean variance optimization uses quantitative models to maximize expected return, given a certain level of portfolio risk, or, alternatively, to minimize portfolio risk, given a certain fixed level of expected return. The result of the model has come to be called an "efficient frontier," or the set of possible portfolio allocations that maximizes expected returns for a given level of variance (risk) or minimizes variance (risk) for a given level of return. The model reveals the mathematical appeal of diversification. Mean variance optimization provides some interesting insights into asset allocations that include stocks, bonds, and market-neutral strategies.

The market-neutral strategies derive returns from relationships between securities rather than from the directional bias associated with traditional investments in stocks or bonds. And while those relationships, as a group, are subject to volatility, the returns they produced over the past decade have generally been more stable than, and have had low correlation with, traditional stock and bond indexes. This point is illustrated in Figure 3.1, using mean variance optimization. For each level of risk (standard deviation), the efficient frontier maximizes historical returns, given the allocation options (market-neutral strategies, stocks, bonds).

All of the points on the curve represent "efficient portfolios"— that is, they maximize expected return for a given level of variance,

Figure 3.1   Efficient Frontier: Combined Market-Neutral Strategies,
January 1990–December 1999

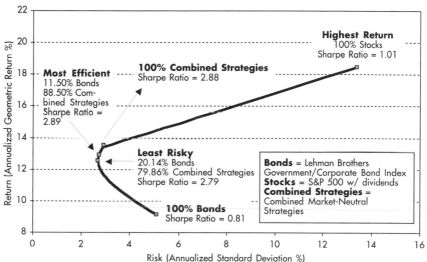

or they minimize variance for a given level of return. No combinations of the inputs can be put together to yield a result to the left of the curve. The set of all possible allocations, including a 100 percent allocation to bonds and a 100 percent allocation to stocks, resides on or inside the frontier. The point with the highest risk-adjusted return, as measured by the Sharpe Ratio, is referred to as the most efficient allocation.

In this case, 100 percent allocation to stocks or bonds represents the upper and lower bounds of the frontier. The most efficient allocation would have been over 88 percent to the aggregate market-neutral index, and about 12 percent to bonds. This is to be expected because the market-neutral index aggregates a number of different strategies that include exposures to a wide range of somewhat uncorrelated asset classes. However, although Figure 3.1 is not meant to recommend allocating 88 percent of a portfolio into market-neutral strategies, the magnitude of improvement in risk-adjusted returns by adding market-neutral strategies should not be overlooked. By increasing the allocation to market-neutral strategies, an investor could achieve a higher return than that from bonds while incurring less risk. Figure 3.2 shows how overall portfolio volatility is reduced (without a corresponding proportional reduction in returns) by adding market-neutral strategies to a traditional portfolio in 10 percent increments. The proportion of stocks to bonds remains fixed at 60/40 (e.g., 20 percent market neutral +48 percent stocks +32 percent bonds = 100 percent).

By adding market-neutral strategies to a traditional portfolio of stocks and bonds, variability could have been reduced dramatically without a proportional decrease in returns. The 100 percent market-neutral portfolio had only one-third the volatility of the traditional portfolio with only one-tenth less return.

Figure 3.2 Improvement in Sharpe Ratio by Adding Combined Market-Neutral Strategies to a 60/40 Portfolio of Stocks/Bonds—January 1990–December 1999

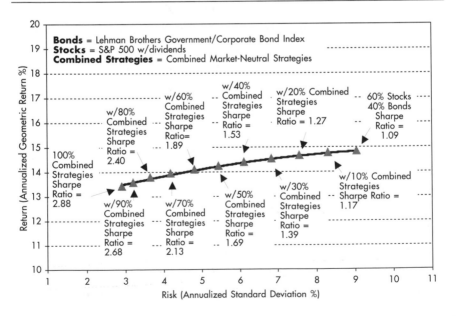

REDUCING EXPOSURE TO RISK

Market-neutral strategies, when added to a portfolio of traditional assets (assumed to be 60 percent stocks and 40 percent bonds), can reduce the overall portfolio's exposure to systemic risk in the market. Systemic risk, referred to as market risk and measured by beta, is the risk common to all securities in a similar asset class (in this case, the stock market). Systemic risk is driven by macroeconomic and investor factors, and therefore is more difficult to remove from portfolios by traditional diversification tactics such as the number of investments, different industries, market capitalization, or investment mix. However, because market-neutral strategies derive their returns from relationships between securities rather than the directional fortunes of an asset class (as occurs with traditional investments in stocks or bonds), the risk-to-return profiles of such strategies have a low correlation to those of the overall market.

As discussed previously, the investment returns generated by traditional portfolio structures can be enhanced on a risk-adjusted basis by allocating a portion of the investment funds to market-neutral strategies. In addition, such an allocation can reduce exposure to stock market risk, as measured by beta.

With a traditional portfolio—consisting of 60 percent stocks, represented by the S&P 500, and 40 percent bonds, measured by the Lehman Brothers Aggregate Government/Corporate Bond Index—the historical return over the past ten years has been 14.73 percent with an accompanying beta of .66. When a portfolio of market-neutral strategies is added to this traditional 60/40 fixed portfolio mix in 10 percent increments (e.g., 20 percent market neutral + 48 percent stocks + 32 percent bonds = 100 percent), market risk, as measured by beta, is reduced, and competitive portfolio returns are maintained (Figure 3.3).

At each level of the systemic risk incurred, the portfolio with an allocation to the market-neutral strategies offers higher returns

Figure 3.3 Market-Neutral Strategies as an Alternative to Bonds,
January 1990–December 1999

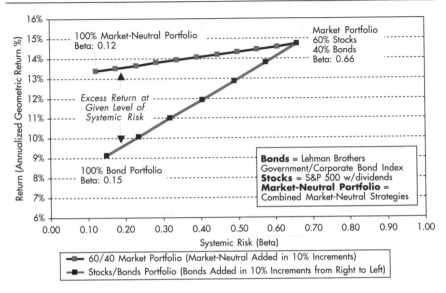

than the traditional portfolio. Figure 3.3 shows that increasing the allocation to bonds reduces systemic risk, but it does so at a greater cost to returns than if the allocation to market-neutral strategies is increased while holding the remainder at a constant 60/40 stocks/bonds mix. At any level to the left of the traditional portfolio mix, a combination of the market-neutral portfolio with the traditional mix produces a superior risk-to-return profile for the combined portfolio because it reduces the systemic risk incurred. The combined portfolio return is reduced by just over 9 percent (from 14.73 percent to 13.38 percent) along this sample of portfolios. However, along this same frontier, systemic risk, as measured by beta, is reduced by over 80 percent (from .66 to .12). This is only possible because the market-neutral strategies extract excess returns from pricing inefficiencies in the market.

Not surprisingly, the return-to-risk attributes produced by combining a market-neutral portfolio with the traditional portfolio mix are superior to those of the traditional portfolio. The Treynor Measure used to gauge this factor is quite similar to the Sharpe Ratio, but variance is replaced with beta in the denominator (Figure 3.4):

$$\text{Treynor Measure} = \frac{\text{Portfolio return} - \text{Risk-free rate}}{\text{Beta}}$$

In Figure 3.4, as exposure to stock market risk is reduced by adding a larger allocation to the market-neutral portfolio, beta declines at a faster rate than the combined portfolio return. This results in a strong upward movement in the Treynor Measure. In addition, the rate at which the Treynor Measure improves as beta is reduced for the combined portfolio is much higher than if the bond allocation were to be increased. By adding a market-neutral portfolio to a traditional 60/40 portfolio mix, it may be possible for investors to generate returns similar to those of a traditional

Figure 3.4 Improvement in Treynor Measure as Market-Neutral Portfolio Is Substituted for Bonds, January 1990–December 1999

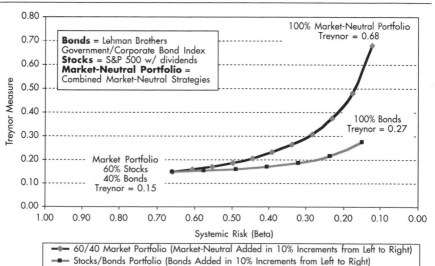

60/40 stock/bond portfolio mix, but with reduced exposure to systemic stock market risk.

Similar results occur when a stocks/bonds portfolio is compared to a stocks/market-neutral portfolio. Again, the S&P 500 is used to represent a portfolio of stocks and the Lehman Brothers Aggregate Government/Corporate Bonds Index is a proxy for bonds. Over the past decade, the S&P 500 has posted an average annual return of 18.45 percent, which is, of course, accompanied by a beta of 1. The bond index has posted returns of 9.14 percent with a beta of .1506 as compared to the S&P 500 Index.

Traditionally, investors would use an allocation of bonds to diversify equity market exposure and achieve less variance in returns. By replacing the allocation of a bond portfolio with an allocation to a portfolio of market-neutral strategies, investors may be able to produce higher returns at a given level of stock market risk.

Figure 3.5 Market-Neutral Strategies as an Alternative to Bonds II, January 1990–December 1999

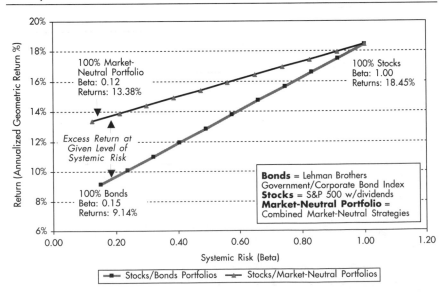

Figure 3.5 shows the two sets of returns at specific levels of systemic risk (beta). The lower line is the traditional mix of stocks and bonds; the upper line replaces bonds with a portfolio of market-neutral strategies. As the graph shifts to the right, the allocation to stocks (which increases market risk) increases in 10 percent increments from zero to 100 percent.

As illustrated in Figure 3.5, at any level of market risk, the portfolio consisting of stocks and the market-neutral strategies provided better return/risk characteristics than the stock and bond portfolio allocations, with the obvious exception of owning the S&P 500, or all of the market risk.

Again, using the Treynor Measure, Figure 3.6 indicates that a portfolio of stocks and the market-neutral strategies produces more return, given a certain level of risk, than combinations of stocks and bonds. As the graph shifts to the right, the allocation to stocks (which increases market risk) decreases in 10 percent increments from 100 to 0 percent.

Figure 3.6 Improvement in Treynor Measure as Market-Neutral Portfolio Is Substituted for Bonds, January 1990–December 1999

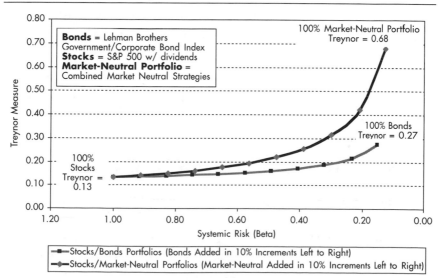

The marginal improvement in the Treynor Measure increases significantly at higher levels of market-neutral allocations, revealing the historical benefit of replacing the bond portfolio with a portfolio of market-neutral strategies. The tactic of beginning at the 70/30 allocation of stocks and the diversifying asset (bonds or the market-neutral portfolio), and then increasing the diversifying asset allocation (moving left-to-right along the graph), increases the marginal return (for a given level of market risk incurred) of the market-neutral combination over the traditional portfolio mix of stock and bonds. By replacing the allocation of a bond portfolio with an allocation to a portfolio of market-neutral strategies, investors may be able to produce higher returns for a given level of market risk.

The various market-neutral and hedged strategies offer returns that are higher than those of fixed income, but they have lower volatility than equities. In addition, these strategies exhibit low correlation to equity and fixed-income indexes in most market environments. Of particular interest, given the hedged nature of these strategies, is performance during periods when the stock market is down. In the 1990s, there were 37 months during which the S&P 500 registered negative returns. The average monthly return of the S&P 500 during these periods was –3.01 percent. The aggregate market-neutral strategies were down in only eight (22 percent) of these months, and they registered an average return of 0.47 percent during the 37 periods. In the following section, the eight primary market-neutral and hedged strategies are briefly introduced.

MARKET-NEUTRAL AND HEDGED STRATEGIES

Convertible Arbitrage

Convertible arbitrageurs (see Chapter 4) construct long portfolios of convertible securities and hedge these positions by selling short the underlying stock of each bond. Convertible securities include convertible bonds, convertible preferred stock, and warrants, but the analysis here is confined to convertible bonds.

Convertible bonds are bonds that can be converted into a fixed number of shares of the issuing company's stock. Because they are hybrid securities that have features of a bond and of stock, their valuations reflect both types of instruments. Typically, the price of the convertible will decline less rapidly than the underlying stock in a falling equity market, and will mirror the price of the stock more closely in a rising equity market. Generally, convertible arbitrageurs extract arbitrage-like profits from these complex pricing relationships by purchasing the convertible bond and selling short its underlying stock. Figure 3.7 shows the efficient frontier for the 1990s with convertible arbitrage, stocks, and bonds as inputs.

Figure 3.7 Efficient Frontier: Convertible Arbitrage, January 1990–December 1999

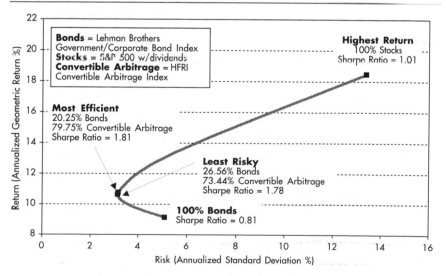

Fixed-Income Arbitrage

Fixed-income arbitrage strategies (see Chapter 5) involve investing in one or more mispriced fixed-income securities, and hedging out underlying market risk with another fixed-income security. Fixed-income arbitrage seeks to capture these, usually small, pricing anomalies while maintaining minimal exposure to interest rates and other systemic market risks. In most cases, fixed-income arbitrageurs take offsetting long and short positions in similar fixed-income securities. The securities' values are mathematically or historically interrelated, but that relationship is temporarily out of sync. These positions could include corporate debt, sovereign debt, municipal debt, or the sovereign debt of emerging market countries. Many trades may involve swaps and futures.

By purchasing cheap fixed-income securities and selling short an equal amount of expensive fixed-income securities, fixed-income arbitrageurs protect themselves from changes in interest rates. If they select instruments that respond similarly to interest rate changes, then an interest rate rise that adversely affects the long position will have an offsetting positive effect on the short position. In fixed-income terminology, they do not make directional duration bets. They realize a profit when the skewed relationship between the securities returns to normal. Rather than try to guess the direction in which the market will go, they neutralize interest rate changes and derive profit from their ability to identify similar securities that are mispriced relative to one another.

Because the prices of fixed-income instruments are based on yield curves, volatility curves, expected cash flows, credit ratings, and special bond and option features, managers must use sophisticated analytical models to identify true pricing disparities. The complexity of fixed-income pricing is actually essential to fixed-income arbitrageurs. They rely on market events, and on investors less sophisticated than themselves, to create over- and undervalued securities by failing to explicitly value some feature of an

Figure 3.8   Efficient Frontier: Fixed-Income Arbitrage,
January 1990–December 1999

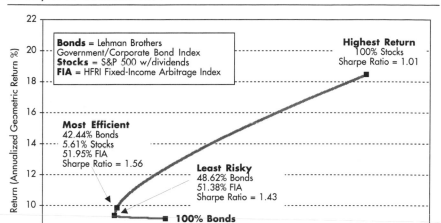

instrument (such as a call option). Figure 3.8 shows the efficient frontier for the 1990s with fixed-income arbitrage and stocks and bonds as inputs.

Mortgage-Backed Securities Arbitrage

Mortgage-backed securities (MBS) arbitrage (see Chapter 6) is essentially a particular kind of fixed-income arbitrage. More specifically, it can be referred to as a type of fixed-income relative value trading. An MBS instrument is a fixed-income security with underlying prepayment options. MBS arbitrage managers use proprietary models to value and rank the embedded options of MBS instruments, and ultimately to rank them by option-adjusted spreads (OAS). The OAS is the average spread over the Treasury yield curve that equates the security's observed market price with a probabilistically derived present value of future MBS cash flows.

The OAS can be interpreted as the security's incremental return over Treasuries, adjusted for the effects of interest rate volatility and its impact on the MBS's prepayment tendencies. The securities that offer the best value are bought and hedged to zero duration using Treasuries, Treasury options, futures, caps, floors, swaps, and forward contracts. By maintaining zero duration, managers avoid making unwanted bets on the direction of interest rates and concentrate on deriving returns from security valuation and selection. Mortgage managers can be distinguished by the sector of the MBS market they invest in (there are many different kinds of MBS structures with customized risk-and-return characteristics), by the valuation systems they use, and by their risk management or hedging practices. Figure 3.9 shows the efficient frontier for the period from 1993 through the end of 1999, with MBS arbitrage and stocks and bonds as inputs.

Figure 3.9 Efficient Frontier: Mortgage-Backed Securities Arbitrage, January 1993–December 1999

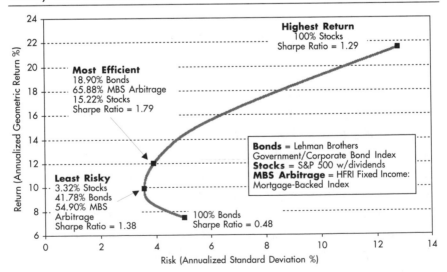

Merger Arbitrage

Merger arbitrage (see Chapter 7) usually involves buying the common stock of a company that is being acquired by or is merging with another company, and selling short the stock of the acquiring company. Some managers may use options rather than stock, if it is cheaper to achieve the trade in that fashion. The target company's stock will typically trade at a discount to the value that it will attain after the merger is completed. The discount is available because: (1) corporate acquisitions are generally made at a premium to the stock price of the target company prior to the announcement of the proposed merger, and (2) all mergers involve event risk—that is, risk that the transaction will fail to be completed as announced. If the transaction fails to be completed, then the price of the target company's stock usually declines—sometimes, dramatically. Merger arbitrage specialists make profits when they correctly anticipate the outcome of an announced merger and lock in the spread between the current market price of the target company's stock and the amount offered by the acquiring firm.

If the announced deal goes through, stock in the target company will become an ownership interest in the acquiring company. In theory, then, the two stocks can be seen to represent ownership interests in the same company. But until the deal is consummated, the prices of the two stocks will usually reflect the market's uncertainty about whether the deal will go through. Uncertainty can be generated by any number of factors; they include but are not confined to: financing difficulties, regulatory roadblocks, collars, management issues, market sentiment, and the emergence of new negative information about one of the two firms. Often, this means that the target company's stock will trade at a discount to the value it will attain if the deal is completed. Merger arbitrage specialists will usually translate an arbitrage spread into an annualized rate of return, estimate the probability that the deal will go through, and then determine whether the returns to be derived from the spread—if the deal is completed—offer sufficient compensation for the estimated risk of the deal's failing.

Merger arbitrage specialists do not try to anticipate possible merger activity, because that approach would be tantamount to investing on the basis of rumors. Instead, they research announced mergers and acquisitions as a way of reducing their uncertainty about each of the possible outcomes. Before taking a position, they will consider public corporate documents of the firms, earlier years' financial statements for each of the firms, EDGAR[1] Fed filings, analysts' reports, standard media releases, conference calls and conversations with the companies, and industry contacts. If they feel that the rate of return implicit in the spread is significantly more than the actual risk if the deal fails to be completed, then they will invest in the situation. Generally, they will add to positions as more non-negative information becomes available, as market sentiment toward the deal solidifies, and as the outcome of the transaction becomes more certain. A merger arbitrage manager will liquidate an investment position when new negative information is uncovered and the return is no longer a sufficient reward for the perceived risks of holding the position. But if all goes as planned, the position will not be liquidated until the transaction is consummated. Figure 3.10 shows the efficient frontier for the 1990s, with merger arbitrage and stocks and bonds as inputs.

Equity Hedge

Equity hedge (see Chapter 8) is not properly a market-neutral strategy, but it is included here for purposes of comparison and because the strategy's hedging philosophy has much in common with

---

[1] Electronic Data Gathering, Analysis, and Retrieval.

Figure 3.10 Efficient Frontier: Merger Arbitrage, January 1990–December 1999

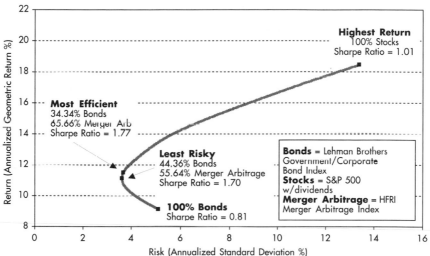

market-neutral strategies. Equity hedge managers build equity portfolios that combine core long holdings with short sales of stock or stock index options. Their net market exposure (long positions/short positions) will vary, depending on the manager's preference and the market conditions. Ideally, they would increase long exposure in a bull market and decrease it, or even be net short, in a bear market. The short exposure is usually intended to act as a hedge against a general stock market decline, but many managers hope to generate an ongoing positive return from their short positions.

In a rising market, well-chosen long positions will increase in value as fast as or faster than the market, and well-chosen short positions will increase less than the long positions or will even decline in value. Similarly, in a declining market, well-chosen short holdings tend to fall more rapidly than the market falls, and well-chosen long holdings fall less rapidly than the market or even increase in value. Underperforming short positions reduce returns in a rising market, but this decrease in returns is accepted by

Figure 3.11   Efficient Frontier: Equity Hedge, January 1990–December 1999

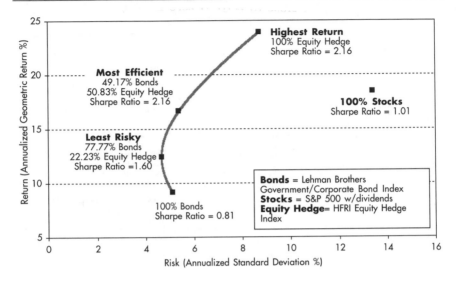

equity hedge managers in exchange for the protection the short positions provide in a declining market. The source of return for the long side of the portfolio is similar to that of traditional stock pickers, but the source of return for the strategy as a whole differs in the use of short selling and hedging to outperform the market in a declining or downward trending market. Thus, in a bull market, equity hedge managers should achieve positive but smaller returns than if they were long only; in a bear market, they may have negative returns, but less than if they were long only. Therefore, one can expect equity hedge managers to make returns, over time, that are similar to those of long-only managers, but with less volatility. Figure 3.11 shows the efficient frontier for the 1990s, with equity hedge and stocks and bonds as inputs.

Equity Market Neutral and Statistical Arbitrage

Equity market-neutral managers (see Chapter 9) will usually hold a large number of long equity positions and an equal, or close to equal, dollar amount of offsetting short equity positions, so that their total net exposure is close to zero. A zero net exposure—referred to as "dollar neutrality"—is common to all equity market-neutral strategies. By going long and short in equal amounts, the equity market-neutral manager seeks to "neutralize" any effect, on his or her portfolio, from a systemic change in a variable or from investor sentiment that affects valuations of the stock market as a whole. Some, but not all, equity market-neutral managers will extend the concept of neutrality to risk factors, subsets, or characteristics such as beta, industry, sector, investment style, and market capitalization. In all equity market-neutral portfolios, stocks expected to outperform the market are held long, and stocks expected to underperform the market are sold short. Returns are derived from the long/short spread, or the amount by which long positions outperform short positions. Thus, equity market-neutral managers, in theory, will be able to achieve stable returns, regardless of the overall direction of the stock market.

Figure 3.12 Efficient Frontier: Equity Market Neutral, January 1990–December 1999

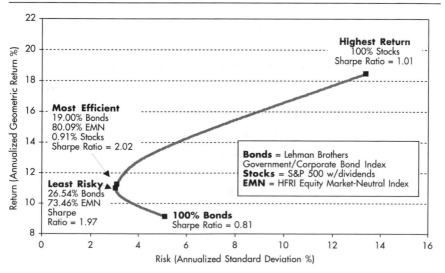

In a general sense, statistical arbitrage (see Chapter 9) is differentiated from equity market neutral by the constraints it places on managers' discretion. Different managers allow for different amounts of human discretion, but even among the most quantitatively oriented managers, an "art" is involved in building and refining models and in the constant process of iteration that is required to keep the model alive and dynamic. The different approaches are the same in that equal dollar amounts of stocks on the long side and the short side protect against systemic directional moves in the prices of stock. They differ in the method of getting to that portfolio. Figure 3.12 on page 49 shows the efficient frontier for the 1990s, with equity market neutral and stocks and bonds as inputs. Figure 3.13 shows the efficient frontier for the 1990s, with equity statistical arbitrage and stocks and bonds as inputs.

Figure 3.13   Efficient Frontier: Equity Statistical Arbitrage, January 1990–December 1999

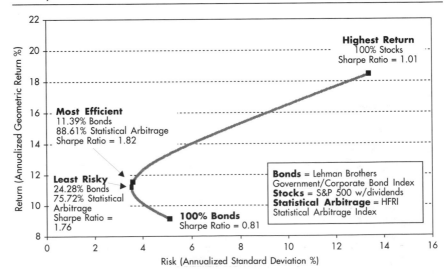

Relative Value Arbitrage

Relative value arbitrage managers (see Chapter 10) are usually practitioners of multiple strategies. Their overall emphasis is on making "spread trades"—trades that derive returns from the relationship between two related securities—rather than on the direction of the market. Generally, relative value arbitrageurs take offsetting long and short positions in similar or related securities with values that are mathematically or historically interrelated, but where that relationship is temporarily distorted. They realize a profit when the skewed relationship between the securities returns to normal.

Rather than try to guess the direction in which the market will go, managers neutralize their overall position by taking both long and short positions. In addition, relative value managers add value by determining which relative value strategies offer the best

Figure 3.14 Efficient Frontier: Relative Value Arbitrage,
January 1990 December 1999

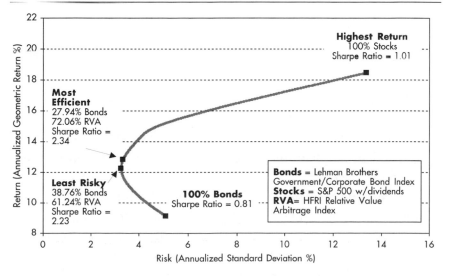

opportunities at any given time, and weighting those strategies accordingly in their overall portfolio. Relative value strategies may include forms of fixed-income arbitrage: mortgage-backed arbitrage, merger arbitrage, convertible arbitrage, statistical arbitrage, pairs trading, options and warrants trading, capital structure arbitrage, and structured discount convertibles that are more commonly known as Regulation D securities. Figure 3.14 on page 51 shows the efficient frontier for the 1990s, with relative value arbitrage and stocks and bonds as inputs.

ACHIEVING SUPERIOR RISK-ADJUSTED RETURNS

The evidence put forth thus far in this chapter supports the claim that market-neutral strategies can provide risk-adjusted returns that are superior to those of traditional investments (returns higher than those offered by bonds, but with lower variability than either stocks or bonds). All of the strategies included in the analysis have been able to do so by using relationship investing to extract returns from pricing inefficiencies in the marketplace.

ASSESSING THE RISKS

Hedge fund investors are exposed to two basic types of risk: (1) risks associated with the investment strategy, and (2) risks associated with accessing that strategy. Like any investment strategy, a hedge fund strategy involves risks that are specific to the strategy and the markets it is exposed to, and risks that can be attributed to the particular style of the manager, such as use of leverage or hedging techniques.

Assuming that the strategy risks are understood by the investor and deemed acceptable, there is still the risk of accessing the strategy. Usually, such risks are attributable to "blind" investing—investing in a fund that does not provide adequate information to investors about its operations, and does not allow the investors custody of the invested assets. In such a situation, investors are left without information and control of their investment, and may find it difficult to hold the fund manager accountable for his or her investment decisions.

In the 1990s, it was often easy to ignore these issues. However, the high-profile coverage and subsequent bailout of Long Term Capital Management (LTCM) in 1998 brought them to the forefront of risk management. It is now understood that LTCM operated in a manner that was not indicative of most other managers' strategies, much less the strategies of the broader industry. The lessons learned should be kept in mind when considering any investment opportunity. They include:

1. Leverage can increase risk.
2. Investing blindly makes it difficult to assess exposure to risks.
3. Past performance is not indicative of future results.
4. All long exposures become correlated when liquidity dries up.
5. Many hedge fund strategies are value-based and do not perform well in a momentum environment.

These risks can best be addressed by understanding the investment approach at the outset and conducting ongoing monitoring of the portfolio. Investors can avoid the risks of blind investing by accessing the manager's talent through a separately managed account, which, by definition, gives the investor both access and control of his or her assets. With proper controls and oversight, most concerns should be alleviated. If the investment is made through a commingled fund, there are additional control and custody issues, but the best approach includes daily portfolio transparency and monitoring of predefined investment parameters.

Investors should identify and evaluate investment parameters prior to making an allocation. In the due diligence process—that is, the process of gathering and analyzing information about an investment opportunity—an investor will consider factors such as what markets and instruments are used; concentrations; source of returns; pricing; repeatability of returns; buy and sell disciplines; key personnel; market capitalization; manager capacity; and the market environment. Investment decisions are based, at least in part, on some combination of these factors. Establishing investment parameters also involves constraining some factors.

Investment objectives and parameters should be defined prior to the allocation and based on careful consideration of factors that may influence the investment and the profile of the assets to be invested. As these factors change over time, investors should reconsider their original investment rationale. To do so, they need a method for monitoring the changes. Factors that relate to investment parameters can be monitored through an ongoing review of the portfolio. This level of access to information is known as transparency.

TRANSPARENCY

Transparency is the ability to review—that is, "look through"—a manager's portfolio and identify the factors that must be considered when making prudent investment decisions. Usually, the term refers to the ability to review the underlying instruments and positions. It is particularly important for market-neutral investments because the multiple dimensions created by long and short positions, leverage, and the use of derivatives require constant oversight.

Three things should be kept in mind regarding transparency.

1. Ideally, the relevant transaction information should come from a third party, such as the prime broker or custodian, rather than from the manager.

2. The instruments should be priced independently and not by the manager. Prime brokers often follow managers' directions, so position information from third-party sources can sometimes reflect managers' marks. Prices should be independently verified whenever possible.

3. In some strategies, this level of transparency may be achievable, but others do not allow daily valuation, and some managers will not agree to this level of transparency.

Daily transparency, which first emerged as a tool to monitor risk, also makes daily pricing possible. This, in turn, has opened the door to new products and structures for accessing hedge fund strategies, such as mutual funds and strategy index funds. Hedge Fund Research (HFR) and Zurich Capital Markets (ZCM) have recently launched a set of strategy pure, fully transparent, daily priced, nonleveraged indexes for a number of hedge fund strategies.[2] They were developed to capture the core, nonleveraged return generated by each strategy, and to respond to the institutional demand for better tools for indexing alternative managers.

An increasing number of institutions believe that prudent investing requires transparency at the portfolio level to understand risk-and-reward characteristics of the investment and to prevent drift into higher risk exposures, whether through higher leverage or lower-quality investments. There is also a growing interest in strategies with identifiable and repeatable sources of return.

FOCUSING ON THE UNDERLYING STRATEGIES

Chapters 1 through 3 have made plain the growing importance of market-neutral strategies. First, evidence of the dramatic growth of

---

[2] This information is currently available online through various sources, including Bloomberg, Bridge, and www.hfr.com.

hedge funds—the domicile of many of the foremost practitioners of market-neutral strategies—during the past decade was traced, along with some of the important factors driving that growth. Second, it was shown that, while hedge fund assets in general have been on the rise, allocations to market-neutral strategies represented a much larger proportion of those assets in 1999 than they did in 1990. The flow of funds to market-neutral investment strategies indicates investor demand for relationship-based investment strategies that provide downside protection. Third, the discussion pointed out the changing nature of hedge fund investors—in particular, the increased interest and allocations from institutional investors.

Fourth, linear analysis and mean variance optimization were used to show the benefits that can be gained from diversification—that is, from making allocations to market-neutral strategies within a traditional portfolio of stocks and bonds. Fifth, a brief overview of the market-neutral strategies was provided. Lastly, the risks associated with accessing hedge fund strategies were discussed—particularly, problems that derive from blind investments. Through separate accounts, transparent investments in commingled funds, or an investment in newly emerging transparent strategy indexes, these risks can be minimized.

Each of these trends lends support to the view that it is becoming increasingly important to concentrate on the underlying strategies themselves. Accordingly, Chapters 4 through 10 focus readers' attention on detailed discussions of market-neutral strategies.

Convertible Arbitrage   4

Convertible arbitrageurs construct long portfolios of convertible securities and hedge these positions by selling short the underlying stock of each bond. Convertible securities include convertible bonds, convertible preferred stock, and warrants. The discussion here is limited to convertible bonds, but the concepts are applicable to all convertible securities. Convertible bonds are bonds that can be converted into a fixed number of shares of the issuing company's stock. They are hybrid securities that have features of a bond and of a stock; therefore, their valuations reflect both types of instruments. Generally, the price of the convertible security will decline less rapidly than the underlying stock in a falling equity market and will mirror the price of the stock more closely in a rising equity market. Typically, convertible arbitrageurs extract arbitrage-like profits from these complex pricing relationships by purchasing the convertible bond and selling short its underlying stock.

CONVERTIBLE BOND VALUATION

Before delving into the kinds of trades that convertible arbitrageurs execute, it is important to understand the different components that determine a convertible bond's value and the sometimes complex models that managers use to value them.

Statistical Advantage

If an investment manager can identify a convertible bond with a favorable total return profile, then that manager can make arbitrage profits by purchasing the convertible bond and selling short the underlying stock. The price of a convertible bond with a favorable return profile will decline less rapidly than the price of the underlying stock. In a rising equity market, the price of the convertible bond will be more highly correlated to the price of the stock. The comparative returns in Table 4.1 illustrate these relationships.

Table 4.1   Total Annual Return Profile

Change in Price of Underlying Equity	Down 10%	Unchanged	Up 10%
Common stock, percent of change	−10	0	+10
Convertible bond, percent of change (with coupon)	−2	+5	+8

The total return profile of the convertible bond is favorable because it captures most of the upward movement of the underlying equity but escapes a lot of the downside. For the sake of simplicity, we will assume, for now, that the equity does not pay a dividend, so it returns 0 percent if its price does not change. On the other hand, the convertible bond returns 5 percent because it pays a coupon. In addition, the equity and the convertible bond do not respond equally to changes in the price of the equity. These two features give the convertible bond a statistical advantage.

Mathematically, an investment manager who invests in a non-dividend-paying equity security gets a risk-to-reward relationship that has no inherent edge. This is not to say that good stock pickers will not make money on stocks; with everything else held equal, statistically speaking, a stock has just as much potential to decline as it has to appreciate. This simply means that a 10 percent movement in either direction produces a similar percentage of gain or loss, and is expressed as a 1:1 reward-to-risk potential. The convertible bond's reward-to-risk potential in Table 4.1 is 4:1 because a 10 percent move in either direction produces gain potential that is four times the potential loss.

Convertible Valuation Components

Investment Value

The valuation of convertible bonds is a hybrid of stock and bond valuation, because the convertible combines features of both the stock and the bond. The value of the bond component of a convertible is known as the investment value. In spite of the name, investment value should not be confused with the market value of the convertible security. It refers solely to the fixed-income component of the security: the value of the bond, stripped of the option to convert to stock.

The investment value represents a sort of floor for the investment. The price of the convertible will not normally fall below its investment value because, even if the stock component falls significantly, the convertible retains its value as a bond. The only exception is when the issuing company runs into fundamental difficulties that cause the stock price to fall rapidly and cause the credit quality of the bond component to come into question. These types of securities, known as busted convertibles, will be discussed later in this chapter. Convertible arbitrageurs will use the tools of conventional fixed-income analysis—such as fundamental analysis, coupon and maturity date, credit quality, and yield to maturity—to determine the investment value of a convertible bond.

Theoretically, the investment value of a convertible bond will remain stable over a wide range of stock prices, as long as interest rates remain unchanged. If the stock price approaches zero, the investment value will generally follow because plummeting stock prices are a sign of financial distress within the company and may lead to possible bankruptcy and default on debt. On the other hand, the investment value of the bond should not be influenced by increasing stock prices, although the overall market price of the convertible will be affected. This is based on the assumption that the creditworthiness and financial condition of issuing companies, which are key factors in determining the investment value of the convertible bond, will change slowly, and the investment value should remain unchanged as long as the company's creditworthiness remains intact. In practice, this is usually the case, but dramatic changes in company fundamentals do sometimes occur. A negative earnings surprise will have a negative effect on the investment value of a convertible bond in the same way that a rating downgrade will negatively affect the value of a corporate bond. Deteriorating fundamentals signal an increased risk that the company will not be able to pay the coupon or the principal.

Changes in interest rates will affect the investment value of a convertible bond, just as they affect normal corporate bonds of similar credit quality. Interest rates represent the price of borrowing money. When rates increase, lenders will be attracted to the higher rates, and the value of debt issued at a lower rate will decline. Thus, an increase in interest rates will result in a decline in the investment value of a convertible bond. A decrease in interest rates will have the opposite effect.

It is worth noting once again that a convertible bond's valuation is dynamic and that, under certain circumstances, some components of that price may have more influence than others do. Thus, in a rising interest rate environment, when the investment value of the security is falling, that decline may be overshadowed in the overall price of the convertible because the price of the underlying stock is rising. Typically, a convertible trading at or near its investment value will be more sensitive to changes in interest rates than a convertible trading at a premium to that value (which will be more sensitive to changes in the price of the underlying stock).

Investment Premium

A convertible bond's investment premium is the difference between the market value of the convertible and its investment value. It is expressed as a percentage of the investment value. The calculation disaggregates the embedded bond component of the convertible from the aggregate convertible, and isolates the amount, above and beyond the investment value, that an investor must pay to receive the aggregate hybrid security. For a convertible bond with a par value of $1,000 and an investment value of $800, the investment premium would be (1,000 – 800)/800, or 25 percent. This value is an important measure of downside risk that can be monitored as prices and other variables change. The relevant equation is:

$$\text{Investment premium} = \frac{\text{Market price} - \text{Investment value}}{\text{Investment value}}.$$

Generally, a large investment premium means that a convertible will be very sensitive to changes in the price of the underlying stock. Large investment premiums reflect a large difference between the market value of the convertible and its investment value (caused by a high stock price). As discussed in more detail later in this chapter, when the price of the underlying stock increases, convertibles tend to trade more like the stock than the bond. Thus, if the stock price begins to tumble, the convertible will continue to reflect the decline of the underlying stock until it gets closer to the investment value and begins to reflect the bond component rather than the stock component. By the same logic, a convertible with a small investment premium will be relatively more bond-like and more sensitive to factors that affect the price of bonds, such as changes in interest rates.

Conversion Price

The conversion price is the price the investor receives to convert the bond to stock with the convertible bond at par. When it is issued, a convertible will specify the amount of common stock that is equivalent to the value of the convertible bond at par. This is known as a *conversion ratio*. The conversion price is essential because it determines the number of shares that each bond can be converted into at par (the conversion ratio). However, convertibles rarely trade exactly at par, and the price of the underlying stock is prone to fluctuation.

Conversion Ratio

The conversion ratio is the number of shares of common stock a convertible bondholder would receive, per bond, upon converting the bond to the underlying stock. As stated above, at issuance, it is the number of shares the bondholder would receive at the conversion price if the bond was trading at par. The conversion ratio is fixed for the life of the bond.

$$\text{Conversion ratio} = \frac{\text{Par value}}{\text{Conversion price}}.$$

Conversion Value

The conversion value of a convertible bond represents the value of the equity side of the convertible. It is simply the value of the bond, at any given time, if it were converted to the underlying common stock at the current market price. The value is equal to the number of shares into which each bond can be converted (as specified at issuance), multiplied by the current market price of the common stock. The conversion value, like the investment value, represents a price floor. The convertible should not trade below that price.

$$\text{Conversion value} = \text{Conversion ratio} \times \text{Price of common stock}.$$

Premium Over Conversion Value

Investors are usually willing to pay a premium above a convertible bond's conversion value because the bond features of a convertible provide downside protection and usually yield higher current income, in the form of interest payments, than the stock dividend. The premium is calculated by taking the difference between the market price of the convertible and its conversion value, and dividing it by the conversion value.

$$\text{Conversion premium} = \frac{(\text{Price of convertible} - \text{Conversion value})}{\text{Conversion value}}.$$

A convertible bond's premium over conversion value is the amount the investor pays for the convertible bond in excess of the amount that would be received if the bond were converted into the underlying common stock. In essence, it represents the value of the option to convert the bond to stock. For example, if a bond trading at $1,000 (normal par value) can be converted into 50 shares of a $14 stock, then the conversion value would be $700. The premium is the difference between the price at which the bond is trading when it is purchased and the conversion value, or $300 ($1,000 − $700). The conversion premium is usually expressed as a percentage of the conversion value. Thus, in this example, the convertible bond had a 42.9 percent conversion premium ($300/$700).

Generally, the higher a convertible bond's conversion premium, the less the price of the convertible bond will correlate with the price of the underlying common stock, and the more it will correlate with its investment value. Following the logic described above, it makes sense that the value of the investor's option to convert the bond to stock decreases, and the premium paid for that option decreases when the price of the underlying stock rises and the bond trades more like the stock. As a bond trades closer to its investment value, the equity component becomes less valuable. However, it is important to keep in mind that various factors affect a convertible bond's conversion premium. For example, convertibles with higher yields have a higher conversion premium, because the convertible acts more like a bond as it trades closer to the level at which the issuer could issue nonconvertible debt. Thus, in such cases, investors pay more for the current income component than the equity component, regardless of the price at which the common stock may trade.

Dynamic Relationship of the Components

The separate components described in the preceding sections—investment value, investment premium, conversion price, conversion ratio, conversion value, and premium over conversion value—are embedded in the market price of a convertible security. Because it is a hybrid security, a convertible bond will respond to different market forces than its underlying common stock. In fact, there is almost never a one-to-one correspondence between the price of a convertible bond and the price of its underlying common stock. For example, the price of a convertible bond will tend to move inversely to changes in interest rates because of its bond characteristics, whereas its underlying common stock will react to the perceived macroeconomic causes and effects of such interest rate fluctuations.

There is no single formula for calculating the movement of a convertible security as a function of the price of its underlying equity; instead, a range of factors have varying levels of predictive value. Convertible bond specialists make arbitrage profits by identifying pricing disparities between convertible bonds and their underlying equity, and then tightly monitoring the factors that will change these relationships.

Figure 4.1 is an example of a convertible price curve. The price of the underlying stock is on one axis, and the price of the convertible security is on the other. This curve is representative of the

Figure 4.1 Convertible Price Curve

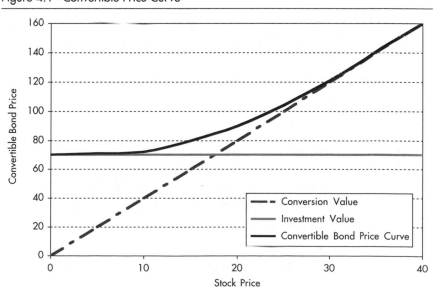

types of curves that convertible arbitrageurs create and examine; however, these curves are not fixed. As illustrated later in this chapter, when the underlying variables contributing to the price of the convertible change, then the shape of the curve can change. In addition, different managers may create different curves for the same security, depending on how they evaluate the relevant variables.

CONVERTIBLE ARBITRAGE APPROACHES

Quantitative Screens

Most convertible arbitrage managers start with a universe of convertible issues and apply a quantitative screen to that universe to identify investment opportunities. Many managers use data obtained from Value Line or from internally generated databases. Managers may screen for different criteria, such as price, coupon, current yield, dividend yield, premium, issue size, duration, or credit rating. Given these and other variables, arbitrage opportunities are identified using evaluation models that locate "theoretically cheap" convertible securities. To identify theoretically cheap securities, managers compare the market value of convertible securities with mathematically calculated expected values of the same convertible, given the market price of the underlying equity securities and other variables such as interest rates, credit quality, implied volatility, and call probability.

Kinds of Hedges

After the arbitrage opportunities are identified, managers determine the appropriate hedge for that security. The standard convertible arbitrage position is neutrally hedged, based on a calculated delta. Delta refers to how the price of a convertible security will respond to a movement in the price of the underlying stock. It is calculated by taking the slope of the tangent line to the convertible price curve at the current price. As noted previously, different managers may create different curves for the same security, so the appropriate delta to maintain neutrality may differ with each manager. Bullish and bearish hedged trades use the same basic strategy but sell short either fewer or more shares of the underlying stock than is necessary for delta neutrality. In the course of fundamental research, a manager may determine that an issuing company will outperform or underperform the market. This opinion is then built into the hedge by selling short either more or less shares than are required for delta neutrality.

Setting Up a Market-Neutral Hedge

In the context of convertible arbitrage, a neutral hedge usually means selling short enough shares of common stock so that, ideally, the position will not incur losses from equity price fluctuations in either direction. Convertible arbitrage managers use sophisticated valuation models and "what if" scenarios to determine the correct number of shares that must be sold short to establish a neutral position. Some of the valuation methodologies that managers use, and the dynamics of maintaining neutrality in real-time trading, are described later in this chapter. For now, it should be emphasized that managers compare the market value of securities with mathematically calculated expected values, given the market price of the underlying equity securities.

The sources of return on a neutral hedge include:

- Interest income from the convertible security purchased.
- Interest earned on cash proceeds from the short sale of the underlying common stock.
- The value of the option to convert, or the conversion premium.

▪ Trading profits from rebalancing the position due to a decline in price of the underlying common stock and/or a rise in the convertible market price.

Example of an Unleveraged Neutrally Hedged Convertible Position

The following example, offered by a practitioner of convertible arbitrage, shows how one manager constructed a neutrally hedged convertible position:

Synetic, Inc.

Evaluation date:	3/1/99
Original issue size:	$150 million
Face amount per bond:	$1,000
Coupon:	5% per annum
Call price	$1028.60 per bond
Call date	July 15, 2000
Maturity:	February 15, 2007
Bond rating:	B/B2
Bond price:	$896.25 per bond
Common stock price:	$43.125 per share
Conversion ratio:	16.667 common shares per bond
Conversion value:	$718.80
Conversion premium:	24.70%
Investment premium:	20.99%
Stock historical volatility:	40.00%
Implied volatility	32.81%

Based on these data, along with assessments of the issuing company's option to call the security, the manager estimated the theoretical value of the security at \$917.90 per bond, or \$22.15 more than its current price. The manager then considered the statistical return profile for the security one year from the date of evaluation, given different possible changes in the price of the underlying stock and taking into account time decay (the contraction of the premium as the convertible approaches expiration). Table 4.2 shows the possible outcomes.

Table 4.2   One-Year Risk vs. Reward

Change in Price of Common Stock	Down 50%	Down 25%	Unchanged	Up 25%	Up 50%
Common stock price	21.56	32.34	43.13	53.91	64.69
Common stock %	−50.00	−25.00	0.00	25.00	50.00
Convertible bond price	76.13	81.17	88.53	100.23	114.17
Convertible %	−15.06	−9.44	−1.22	11.83	27.39
Convertible % (including income)	−9.48	−3.86	4.36	17.41	32.97

The return profile of this convertible bond has upside potential that is disproportionate to the potential downside on a standalone basis. Given this profile, the manager determined that this convertible bond has an attractive risk/reward structure. However, there was still downside risk. To minimize that risk, the manager set up a market-neutral hedge by selling shares of the common stock short, as described below.

Mechanics of Setting Up the Market-Neutral Hedge

A market-neutral hedge is a hedged position that does not favor an upward or a downward move in the underlying stock. The hedge is set up so that the investor is ambivalent regarding the direction of a stock move.

To set up the hedge in this example properly, the short position was created so that small changes in the stock price created a zero profit or loss on the hedge position. This was accomplished by shorting a percentage of the underlying stock shares, based on the convertible bond's current sensitivity to the price of the underlying stock. The current stock sensitivity is best measured by delta, which, as noted previously, is the slope of the tangent line to the convertible curve at the current price. The position for this particular issue was:

Bonds long	100
Conversion ratio	16.6667
Total conversion shares	1,666.67 (Bonds long × Conversion ratio)
Delta	0.54
Appropriate hedge	900 shares (Total conversion shares × Delta)

As a result of this calculation of delta, a hedge was set up with 100 bonds long and 900 shares of common stock sold short:

Return Analysis

Bonds long	100
Stock short	900
Delta	0.54
Hedge	54.00%
Short interest rebate	4.50%
Static yield	7.53%

The manager then analyzed the return profile of the convertible if held for one year, to account for current income, time decay, and profits derived from adjusting the hedge, given movements in the price of the underlying stock (Table 4.3).

Table 4.3   One-Year Risk vs. Reward

Change of Price of Common Stock	Down 50%	Down 25%	Unchanged	Up 25%	Up 50%
Common stock price	21.56	32.34	43.13	53.91	64.69
Convertible bond price	76.13	81.17	88.53	100.23	114.17
Hedge Component Returns (%)					
Convertible income	5.58	5.58	5.58	5.58	5.58
Net short interest	1.46	1.71	1.95	2.19	2.44
Hedge profits	6.59	1.39	-1.22	1.01	5.74
Total return	13.64	8.67	6.31	8.78	13.75

Source: John Zerweck of Zazove Associates, LLC.

The actual annualized return for the period from March 1 to July 30, 1999, was as follows:

Current yield	5.58%
Short stock rebate	1.59%
Trading gains from stock adjustments the stock price ranged from 41.5 to 100.5)	2.08%
Bond price gain (convergence to fair value)	1.53%
Total annualized return	11.14%

Setting up a Bullish Hedge

A bullish hedge, sometimes known as a long-biased hedge, is a hedge in which the manager has sold short fewer shares than are required to maintain neutrality to movements in the price of the underlying stock. By doing so, the manager increases the downside risk but is able to participate more fully in increases in the price of the convertible, which result from increases in the price of the underlying stock. Often, while doing fundamental research, managers uncover information that leads them to believe that the company's stock price will increase. Such information typically may include earnings growth potential, increased cash flow, or indications of solid management. It is important to note that, for most arbitrageurs, a bullish hedge would be justified only when such positive fundamental information has been identified or when a statistical mispricing occurs between the convertible and its underlying equity.

The sources of return for a bullish hedge are similar to those for a neutral hedge, except that a bullish hedge position will participate disproportionately in gains resulting from an increased stock price, and in losses resulting from a decreased stock price.

Setting Up a Bearish Hedge

Sometimes known as a short-biased hedge, a bearish hedge is one for which the manager has sold short more shares than are required to maintain neutrality to movements in the price of the underlying stock. By selling more shares short, managers decrease their participation in increases in the price of the convertible, which result from increases in the underlying stock. At the same time, they benefit more from declining stock prices. Essentially, the manager trades some of the convertible upside for a short stock exposure that will benefit from declines in the stock price. As noted in the preceding discussion of bullish hedges, while managers are doing fundamental research on a company, they often uncover information that leads them to believe that the company's stock price will move (in this case, will decline). Such information may include: indications of management shortcomings, accounting problems, or increased competition.

The sources of return for this type of hedge are similar to the source of return for a neutral hedge except that a bearish hedged position will participate disproportionately in gains resulting from a decreasing stock price and losses resulting from increasing stock prices.

RISKS AND RISK CONTROL

Fundamental Analysis

The degree to which an arbitrage manager engages in fundamental analysis is one factor that defines a manager's style. Certain portions of the convertible market (for example, so-called busted convertibles) and some kinds of hedges (such as bullish or bearish hedges) demand that managers engage in in-depth, traditional, fundamental analysis of the issuing company. If the credit quality of the company is dubious, traditional credit analysis is needed, and if a company shows signs of explosive growth, traditional fundamental stock analysis is generally required. Some managers may do a fundamental analysis of every security in their portfolio. In any case, fundamental analysis is usually one part of a larger process. The amount of fundamental research managers are able to do usually depends on the number of securities in their portfolio and the amount of resources at their disposal.

Traditional Credit Analysis Applicable to Convertible Arbitrage

Some convertible managers perform traditional credit analysis on issuing companies that are under consideration. The purposes of this analysis are, generally, to review the credit quality of the issuing company in order to ensure that coupon and principal payments will be made, and to determine whether this probability is accurately reflected in the price of the convertible security.

Stable or improving trends in both cash flow and interest coverage are generally indicators of the ability of the issuing company to service its debt. These variables are often compared with the corresponding figures for competitors and with results across industries, to determine whether current trends will continue. Some forward-looking managers run rigorous "what if" scenario tests to determine the effect of changes in different variables on the issuing company's credit quality.

It makes sense that managers who invest in higher-yield, high-conversion premium issues—that is, bonds that trade near their investment value and generate very high current income (also known as busted convertibles)—will want to protect that income stream by researching the issuing company's ability to continue to pay it. The more a convertible trades like a bond, the more important traditional fixed-income credit analysis becomes.

Traditional Fundamental Equity Analysis: Applicability to Convertible Arbitrage

Some convertible managers do traditional qualitative and quantitative fundamental equity analysis of issuing companies that are under consideration. Generally, managers study industry and company dynamics that may act as catalysts for stock price appreciation. In some cases, managers may also be interested in dynamics that would indicate stock depreciation. These kinds of traditional fundamental equity analysis are particularly important if the issue trades—or the manager expects it to trade—in a more equity-like fashion. Common points of analysis include accelerating earnings momentum; upward trends in earnings estimate revisions; cash flow return on capital; price-to-earnings and price-to-book value ratios; changing industry dynamics; new product developments; and corporate developments such as spin-offs, restructurings, and potential merger or acquisition involvement.

It behooves managers who invest in more equity-sensitive convertible issues—that is, low-conversion-premium convertibles with a large investment premium—to engage in fundamental equity analysis. In addition, managers who put on bullish and bearish hedges typically attempt to justify these directional plays with some form of fundamental research.

Hedge Analysis

Determining the Appropriate Hedge

After arbitrage opportunities have been identified, convertible arbitrage managers must determine the appropriate number of shares to sell short to maximize the risk-to-reward ratio of each opportunity. In many cases, managers seek to implement a delta-neutral hedge. As detailed previously, delta refers to a change in the price of the convertible, resulting from a change in the price of the underlying stock. A delta-neutral position, ideally, does not incur losses from equity price fluctuations either up or down.

To determine the correct hedge ratio, managers compare the current market price of the convertible to a mathematically calculated expected value. This expected value can be generated using proprietary valuation models or binomial models. Some managers also use the Black–Scholes option-pricing model. Estimates from multiple models may be consulted as a checking method. The valuation models take into account different variables that affect the price of a convertible security. The most common and powerful variables are the stock price, interest rates, volatility, and time to expiration. Generally, managers will run extensive "what if" scenarios for changes in these major variables, to determine how the price of the convertible would act under such circumstances, and how changes would affect the hedge. This information is used to establish target values for the convertible.

Maintaining the Appropriate Hedge

Maintaining the appropriate hedge requires constant attention. Different variables affecting the price of the convertible change after the initial position has been set, so the manager may have to adjust the hedge in order to maintain delta neutrality. The manager does this by selling more shares short or covering some of the initial short position. The hedge is determined by examining the slope of the convertible price curve and determining the appropriate delta (i.e., the slope of the tangent) at the current price of the convertible. Different managers will come to different conclusions about the appropriate hedge, depending on where on the curve that particular security is trading, and whether an opinion about future price directions is being incorporated into the hedge.

Portfolio Construction

Overall Risk-to-Reward

In addition to assessing the risk-to-reward potential of each particular position, managers usually assess the risk-to-reward implications of the portfolio as a whole. Riskier positions will often be counterbalanced by less risky positions; bullish hedges will be balanced by bearish hedges; investment-grade positions will be paired with noninvestment-grade positions.

Diversification

Convertible managers often try to diversify their risk. By spreading their exposure across risk factors, they reduce the possibility that all of their positions will depreciate at once. For example, it is quite unlikely that a group of companies in the technology sector and another group of companies in the energy sector will be affected equally by a drop in the price of oil. Therefore, managers limit their risk exposure by careful consideration of exposure to factors such as:

- Industry.
- Sector.
- Market capitalization of issuer (liquidity).
- Bond-sensitive convertibles (interest rate risk).
- Stock-sensitive convertibles (stock market risk).
- Credit quality (bankruptcy).
- Implied volatility.
- Event risk.

Sell Disciplines

Positions are "unwound" by selling the convertible bond and buying back the stock sold short. Following are the most common reasons to unwind positions:

1. A theoretically undervalued or cheap position is no longer undervalued.
2. An event (for example, a spin-off) occurs that affects the valuations of the two securities in a manner that is out of line with the manager's expectations.
3. New negative information is uncovered and causes the manager to change expectations.
4. Forced selling arises as a result of unexpected redemptions or a liquidity squeeze.
5. The issuing company calls the bond, forcing conversion.

Liquidity

The convertible market is prone to bad performance during "flight-to-quality" scenarios, when global financial markets are unstable and equity prices free-fall. Yield spreads relative to Treasuries increase when investors pull money out of stocks, convertibles, high-yield debt, and corporate debt in favor of the safety provided by Treasury bonds. These situations can result in a lack of trading liquidity in the convertible market, which then affects convertible prices negatively. The third quarter of 1998 was a good example. With convertible prices falling quickly in late August and early September, bid–ask spreads opened to abnormal levels because few investors were buying these securities. The only sellers were either investors in a panic or managers who were forced to liquidate positions in order to fulfill redemption requests or to respond to margin calls from brokers. Some dealers refused to make markets in securities they had actively traded in the past. The lesson to be learned is that no matter how theoretically attractive a security may be, one must always consider the extreme: Can the position be unwound, and at what cost?

Leverage

Leverage, when it is employed prudently, can amplify the returns available from capturing mispricings between convertible securities and their underlying equities. It can be thought of as a form of interest rate arbitrage whereby funds are borrowed at a rate lower than the combined yield of the convertible bond and the short interest received, less any dividends paid on the common stock. However, leverage increases the volatility and overall risk of a portfolio. Because the amount of capital required to support leverage on any given position is determined by the conversion premium, managers using high delta positions that require high hedge ratios have to put up only a small amount of capital. For the most part, this is a way to amplify returns on low-risk positions. In the unusual circumstance when such convertibles start trading down the curve toward their investment value, as they did in the third quarter of 1998, both the risk of the position and the cost of leveraging it increase. At the extremes, leverage can force a manager to sell a security at an inopportune time in order to meet margin requirements.

SOURCE OF RETURN

No single asset class can be shielded from all financial market risks. Certain strategies that balance short and long positions in related securities do, however, have the ability to shield an investor from particular targeted risks, and thus reduce the volatility of returns and the correlation to the market. Under normal market conditions, a delta-neutral convertible strategy will ideally not incur losses if the price of the underlying stock moves up or down within a defined range.

In a normal market environment, convertible arbitrage returns are based on the relationship between convertible securities and their underlying stock, rather than on the direction of the stock market. This is because convertible arbitrageurs take long positions in convertible securities and sell short the underlying stock in a ratio that benefits from the differing return profiles of the two securities under different market scenarios. Convertible arbitrage returns, therefore, are not strongly correlated to overall stock market movement under most market conditions. This statement is less true, however, in periods of extreme stock market movements. Independent of stock market movements, the convertible market has its own valuation cycles, and they are driven by supply and demand for convertibles. Nonetheless, convertible arbitrage specialists can achieve ample and stable returns over time, based on their ability to evaluate and select undervalued convertible securities and hedge them with the underlying stock, as opposed to the far more random nature of most directional investment strategies.

Convertible Bond Market History[1]

The modern U.S. convertible bond market was created during the 1950s. At that time, the very small market attracted highly leveraged issuers such as airline companies. The securities served to reinforce these companies' capital structures at a lower interest rate than straight debt, with less dilution of the equity base. Holders of these bonds were not particularly well protected, and the securities generally had very long maturities—25 years, on average. Over time, other companies began to issue convertible securities as a way of financing growth. In the 1980s, the market began to grow as companies issued convertibles and other equity-linked securities to supplement subordinated capital instruments.

In 1984, IBM issued a convertible bond as a consideration in its acquisition of ROLM, ushering in a new era of high-grade convertible issues. Other investment-grade companies followed, including Ford, Motorola, International Paper, and U.S. West. Average maturities gradually declined from 25 to 10 years as the creditworthiness of issuing entities improved. About half of convertible issues are now investment-grade. Currently, the average maturity of convertible bonds is five to seven years. Shorter maturities have significantly reduced the downside risk of convertibles, because longer maturities make a convertible's basic investment value very sensitive to fluctuations in interest rates.

---

[1] This brief history draws on Tracy Maitland, "Convertible Market Shouldn't Be Overlooked," *Pensions and Investments*, September 16, 1996; and John Pagli, "Global Convertible Securities Arbitrage," paper presented at *MAR/European Conference on Hedge Fund Investments*, February 23, 1997.

As change occurred in the nature of convertible issuers and the issues themselves, convertible investors were also transformed by changes in the financial landscape. In April 1973, the Chicago Board of Options Exchange expanded its membership and made more instruments available for trade on listed exchanges, including financial futures and options. About a month later, the classic article detailing the Black–Scholes options pricing model first appeared. The use of futures and options led governing bodies to loosen rules regarding short selling and the use of leverage. These legal changes led to increased hedging activity, including stock lending and short interest rebates. A market soon emerged that demanded total return products. Convertible securities were a relatively inefficient pocket in that market because they received little attention from major brokerage houses, and information on new and existing issues was not available. With the inefficiency of the convertible market and the new borrowing innovations, convertible arbitrageurs could make outsized returns by capitalizing on the large spreads that existed at the time.

The market has matured over the past decade as more investors have been attracted by the total return possibilities of convertible arbitrage. In addition, advances in information technology have simplified the use of complicated quantitative valuation models. Practitioners of convertible arbitrage strategies now perform about half of domestic convertible trading. Thus, the market for convertibles has become more efficient. Nevertheless, high total rates of return can still be achieved by skilled managers who are able to respond to new challenges that include premium compression, increased corporate event risk, rising equity sensitivity, and tightening arbitrage spreads. The increased size of the market has also created opportunities, including increased liquidity, diversification possibilities, equity market volatility, and the opportunities presented by high-yield busted convertibles for managers who are willing to do in-depth credit analysis.

RECENT GROWTH AND DEVELOPMENTS IN CONVERTIBLE ARBITRAGE

Convertible arbitrage, as a strategy, quadrupled from 0.5 percent of hedge fund assets in 1990 to over 2 percent in 1999. To put this in perspective, one must remember that the current convertible market is not large enough to support the huge amounts of assets that make up the equity and fixed-income markets.

Because the convertible market is much smaller than either the equity or fixed-income markets, it has its own distinctive characteristics. As the hybrid smaller sibling of these larger markets, the convertible market is particularly sensitive to nervousness and fears that affect these other markets. In contrast to the stock market, which draws a more diffuse investor base, the convertible market is peopled almost entirely by professional investors. As a consequence, when one convertible arbitrageur wants to sell, chances are that others do, too.

The professional nature of the convertible market is contrasted by the presence of more total investors and a lower percentage of sophisticated investors in the stock market. The two markets have, on occasion, decoupled and will likely do so again in the future. September 1998 was a perfect example of this phenomenon. The equity markets rebounded from huge losses in August; the convertible market stayed flat after experiencing similar losses in August. Upward pressure from the stock market on convertible prices was counteracted, in this case, by forced selling within the convertible market to reduce risk and maintain normal levels of leverage.

PERFORMANCE IN ADVERSE MARKET CONDITIONS

Three main types of market conditions present problems for convertible arbitrageurs. The first problem occurs when bond prices are falling and stock prices remain flat. Just such a scenario occurred in

1994, when a 200-basis-point spike in interest rates took place without a corresponding drop in stock prices. The bellwether 30-year Treasury bond lost about 30 percent of its value. Convertible valuations reflected this decrease in their value as a fixed-income security. In most cases, such interest rate hikes would cause stock prices to fall as investors moved money into fixed-income securities that had become more attractive. But, for various reasons, stock prices in that period remained flat for the most part, meaning that the short stock positions of convertible arbitrageurs did not offset the drop in convertible prices.

The second problematic scenario occurs when both the stock price and the investment value of convertible securities are falling. Convertible arbitrage managers usually assume that a convertible bond's investment value serves as a downside floor on the position. However, in the case of a company that experiences extremely poor results and eventually enters bankruptcy and defaults on its debt, both the price of the stock and the price of the convertible will approach zero. Normally, a convertible arbitrage manager would make money on the depreciation of the stock while the bond retained its investment value; but, in the extreme case, the bond is carried down and its investment value becomes questionable. This changes how managers must look at the traditional convertible price curve. Figure 4.2 illustrates how this turn of events, when stock and investment values plummet, changes the convertible price curve.

The convertible market is also prone to bad performance during flight-to-quality scenarios, when global financial markets are unstable and equity prices are in a free fall. Under such circumstances, spreads relative to Treasuries open up as investors pull money out of stocks, convertibles, high-yield debt, and corporate debt in favor of the safety provided by Treasury bonds. These situations can create, in the convertible market, a lack of trading liquidity that negatively affects convertible prices. At the extreme,

Figure 4.2 Convertible Price Curve When Stock and Investment Value Plummet

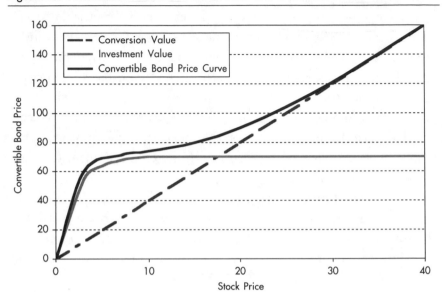

the convertible market can experience a temporary parallel shift in investment values because of widening credit spreads. In this situation, short stock hedges cushion the fall, but the long position in the convertible security falls faster because both its conversion value and its value as a straight bond are dropping. Figure 4.3 illustrates a temporary parallel shift of investment values.

HISTORICAL EXAMPLES

The two most difficult periods for convertible arbitrage in the 1990s were 1994 and the third quarter of 1998. In 1994, bonds were down and stocks were flat—perhaps the worst possible environment for convertible arbitrage. Long positions in convertibles were losing their investment value; straight bond valuations fell, due to rising interest rates; the stock market was flat; and hedges in the underlying stock did not provide a downside cushion. In

Figure 4.3 Convertible Price Curve: Temporary Parallel Shift of Investment Values

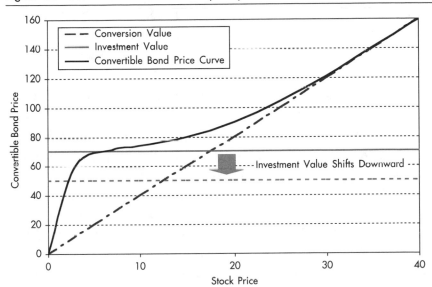

addition, the convertible market was affected by liquidity-driven sell-offs, high convertible premiums, excessive leverage, and spillover effects from derivative disasters. The HFR Convertible Arbitrage Index reflected this difficult environment: the managers included in the Index averaged −3.73 percent returns in 1994.

Coming into August of 1998, convertible valuations were at historic highs. Premium compression throughout the summer and a record-setting stock market had created concerns about overvaluations in the convertible market. Some managers reacted to tighter spreads and stock market exuberance by increasing leverage or lightening hedges. This state of affairs remained latent until the Russian debt crisis created a flight-to-quality situation. Credit spreads immediately blew out as investors pulled funds out of convertibles, high-yield bonds, and corporate bonds. Because of the overriding concern about quality, convertibles began to be priced as junk bonds. This translated into a temporary downward shift in the theoretical investment value of convertibles. Beyond that, the need for liquidity meant that lower-quality issues really had no investment floor. At the same time, stock prices were falling, decreasing the conversion value of convertibles. In such a chaotic period, managers found that premium calculations became very difficult because the normal assumptions made by their valuation models no longer held.

With convertible prices falling quickly at the end of August and the beginning of September, bid–ask spreads opened to abnormal levels because few investors were buying these securities. Sellers included investors in a panic and managers who were forced to liquidate positions in order to fulfill redemption requests or respond to margin calls from brokers. The problem was compounded because of leverage concerns. As the value of their portfolios was decreasing, managers' leverage was increasing, and some of them were forced to sell in order to maintain normal levels of leverage. Leverage concerns only increased when a handful of high-profile

Table 4.4 Returns from Convertible Arbitrage Investments, 1990–1999

Number of Funds	Average Size (Millions of $US)	Year	Jan	Feb	Mar	Apr	May
4	5	1990	−1.47	−0.92	1.26	1.48	1.75
7	6	1991	0.44	1.61	1.39	1.49	0.94
11	7	1992	2.12	0.94	0.99	0.80	1.70
22	14	1993	0.93	0.86	2.19	1.50	1.24
27	20	1994	0.66	0.24	−2.11	−2.79	0.03
32	21	1995	0.55	0.98	1.83	1.90	1.88
33	28	1996	1.82	1.06	1.17	1.88	1.73
35	60	1997	1.01	1.11	0.59	0.68	1.40
52	67	1998	1.91	1.52	1.58	1.35	0.40
55	83	1999	2.11	0.25	1.53	2.66	1.40

* Annual represents geometric compounded average.

managers in the hedge fund industry experienced margin calls. In addition, certain dealers refused to make markets in securities they had actively traded in the past. In essence, dealers became sellers rather than market makers. Managers who were able to avoid selling during this period of depressed prices did not get hurt as badly. The select few who managed to buy during this period made outsized returns in the fourth quarter.

Higher-quality convertible issues returned to normal spread relationships in the first quarter of 1999, and convertible arbitrage performance also rebounded. As in any market downturn, ample opportunities were available to managers who had made it through the difficult period unscathed.

Historical returns for convertible arbitrage funds are shown in Table 4.4. The growth of $1,000 invested in convertible arbitrage (as measured by the HFRI Convertible Arbitrage Index) in 1990 is illustrated in Figure 4.4.

Jun	Jul	Aug	Sep	Oct	Nov	Dec	Annual*
1.72	1.15	−0.18	−0.47	−1.56	−0.05	−0.49	2.16
0.98	1.57	2.09	1.31	1.22	1.66	1.63	17.60
0.71	1.85	1.65	1.46	1.24	0.70	1.09	16.35
1.04	1.41	1.40	1.03	1.29	0.60	0.77	15.22
0.15	1.55	0.80	0.12	−0.09	−0.79	−1.48	−3.73
2.32	2.13	0.96	1.55	1.25	1.58	1.33	19.85
0.44	−0.37	1.40	1.23	1.27	1.40	0.66	14.56
1.71	1.61	1.14	1.11	1.19	0.09	0.41	12.47
0.22	0.49	−3.19	−1.07	−0.48	3.33	1.60	7.77
1.09	1.05	0.42	0.93	0.90	1.80	0.64	15.80

Figure 4.4 Convertible Arbitrage: Growth of $1,000, January 1990–December 1999

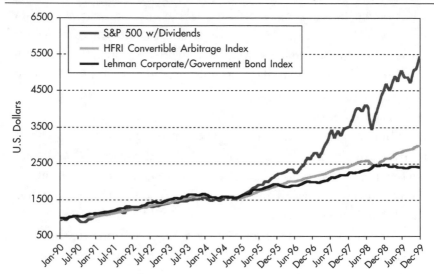

Fixed-Income Arbitrage **5**

Fixed-income arbitrage strategies involve investing in one or more fixed-income securities and hedging against underlying market risk by simultaneously investing in another fixed-income security. These trades seek to capture profit opportunities presented by (usually small) pricing anomalies while maintaining minimum exposure to interest rates and other systemic market risks. In most cases, fixed-income arbitrageurs take offsetting long and short positions in similar fixed-income securities that are mathematically or historically interrelated, when that relationship is temporarily distorted by market events, investor preferences, exogenous shocks to supply or demand, or structural features of the fixed-income market. These positions could include corporate debt, U.S. Treasury securities, U.S. agency debt, sovereign debt, municipal debt, or the sovereign debt of emerging market countries. Often, trades involve swaps and futures.

By purchasing cheap fixed-income securities and selling short an equal amount of expensive fixed-income securities, fixed-income arbitrageurs protect themselves from changes in interest rates that systematically affect the prices of all fixed-income securities. If they select instruments that respond to interest rate changes similarly, then an interest rate rise that adversely affects the long position will have an offsetting positive effect on the short position. In fixed-income terminology, they do not make directional duration bets. They realize a profit when the skewed relationship between the securities returns to a normal range. Rather than try to guess the direction in which the market will go, they neutralize interest rate changes and derive profit from their ability to identify similar securities that are mispriced relative to one another.

Because the prices of fixed-income instruments are based on yield curves, volatility curves, expected cash flows, credit ratings, and special bond and option features, sophisticated analytical models must be used to identify true pricing disparities. The complexity of fixed-income pricing is actually essential to fixed-income arbitrageurs. They rely on market events, investors with different incentives and constraints, investors with different modes of analysis, and investors less sophisticated than themselves, to create relatively over- and undervalued fixed-income securities and, thus, profit opportunities.

FIXED-INCOME ARBITRAGE APPROACHES

Most fixed-income arbitrage trades fit into one of the following categories: basis trades, asset swaps, TED spreads, yield curve arbitrage, and relative value trades. Each is discussed here in detail.

Basis Trades

A basis trade involves the purchase of a government bond and the simultaneous sale of futures contracts on that bond. Bond futures have a delivery option; that is, several different bonds can be delivered to satisfy the futures contract. At expiration, the price of the "cheapest-to-deliver" bond will converge with the price of the futures contract. Because it is not certain which bond will become the cheapest to deliver at maturity, this uncertainty, along with shifts in supply and demand for the underlying bonds, can create profit opportunities.

With their borrowing and lending components, basis trades are profitable when the borrowing becomes cheap relative to the lending. Fixed-income arbitrageurs usually seek out bonds with a price that is relatively low compared to the price of the relevant future. They establish a position and then wait for the cheapest-to-deliver bond to change, knowing all the while that, in the worst-case scenario, they would deliver the currently held bond into the futures contract. Alternatively, a fixed-income arbitrageur would profit if (1) he or she is able to sell short the second or third cheapest-to-deliver bond at a positive net basis (i.e., through cheap financing), and (2) subsequently, the net basis is forced to zero at the expiration of the futures contract because of an insufficient supply of the cheapest-to-deliver bond. In the above example, the insufficient supply of the cheapest-to-deliver bond caused the prices of the second and third cheapest-to-deliver bonds to converge with that of the futures contract. Thus, the fixed-income arbitrageur sold the delivery option for more than it was worth. The following example shows how a basis trade works if the arbitrageur buys the option to deliver.

Example

The 9¼s of 2/15/16 U.S. Treasury bonds traded at a yield pickup of 16.0 basis points to the 11¼s of 2/15/15, which was the cheapest-to-deliver bond for the March 1999 Treasury bond contract. The net basis for the 9¼s of 2/16 was only 6.9/32, representing just 1.5 yield basis points. The dynamic of entering this yield spread through the basis instead of through the spread between both cash bonds allowed a quantifiable downside of just 1.5 basis points (where the 9¼s of 2/16 were delivered into the futures contract). Thus, the manager purchased the delivery option for 1.5 basis points and will participate in any upside that results from an increase in the net basis. Given the coupon differential, underlying swap curve, and liquidity considerations, the manager estimated fair value for the delivery option at closer to 5.5 basis points.

Position Established — 12/21/98	*Position Liquidated — 2/25/99*
Bought 50mm 9 _ ⁹⁄₁₆ @ 143-18	Sold 50mm 9 _ ⁹⁄₁₆ @ 135-17
Sold 570 USH9 @ 128-05	Bought 570 USH9 @ 120-15
Gross Basis* 26/32	Gross Basis* 42.5/32
Net Basis† 6.9/32	Net Basis† 34.6/32

Profit:	Net Basis at Liquidation	34.6/32
	Net Basis When Established	–6.9/32
	Total Profit	**27.7/32**
	Total Profit ($ terms)	27.7/32 × 570 contracts × $31.25 = **$ 493,406**

Hedging Margin per Contract	$ 2,000
Capital Employed (570 contracts × $2,000 less 0% haircut)	**$1,140,000**
Total Return on Capital (66 days)	**43.28%**

---

*Gross Basis = Cash Price – (Conversion Factor × Futures Price)
12/21/98   26/32   = 143-18 – (1.1140 × 128-05)
2/25/99   42.5/32 = 135-17 – (1.1140 × 120-15)
†Net Basis computed using 4.80 percent average Repo rate.
Source: John Carlson, Springfield & Company LLC

Asset Swaps

An asset swap involves an exchange of cash flows between two parties. Usually, the fixed-income arbitrageur purchases a bond and simultaneously swaps the bond's fixed-rate cash flows for the floating-rate cash flows of another (usually, less liquid) security. The difference between the two rates represents the profit opportunity. The risk is that an increase or decrease in interest rates will adversely affect the spread. The trade works only if the floating rate is higher than the financing costs. So, as with basis trades, the trade involves both borrowing and lending, and profit is contingent on the borrowing's being cheap relative to the lending.

When the trade is made with low-risk bonds such as U.S. Treasuries or sovereign issues of major developed nations that are, in essence, default-free, then the relationship between the bond and the swap is likely to be relatively stable. However, changes in tax laws, or a financial or political debacle in the country, can cause such relationships to change. Swaps based on less certain bonds are inherently more risky. Generally, the lowest risk swaps involve swapping a very liquid bond for a less liquid security. Thus, the manager is getting paid to hold a security for which there is little demand. If the demand increases, then the manager can exit the position at a greater profit than anticipated. Otherwise, the security is held to maturity in order to realize the return from the positive spread relative to financing. Because this spread is often quite small, asset swaps are often highly leveraged to produce the desired return.

TED Spreads

"TED" originally referred to *T*reasuries over *E*uro*d*ollars, but now it often refers to all global government bonds hedged against par swaps in the same currency. These trades, which are also called international credit spreads, seek to take advantage of the differences in yields between government securities and LIBOR (London Inter-Bank Offering Rate) contracts of similar maturity.

In the case of Treasuries over Eurodollars, the manager takes a long position in U.S. Treasuries and a short position in Eurodollar contracts of the same maturity. The spread between the two yields is constantly changing and is affected by turmoil or uncertainty in the international financial markets. Generally speaking, positions are established when such spreads are narrow.

For example, if a manager takes a position when the spread is 10 basis points on a three-year bond, the worst-case scenario is that the manager loses 10 basis points per year over the three years. However, the trade anticipates that the spread will widen between the date of the trade and maturity, allowing the manager to exit the trade at a profit. Thus, the manager, in essence, purchases an "option" for 10 basis points to participate in the upside deriving from events that may cause the spread to widen, particularly "flight-to-quality" situations. These situations occur when a large number of investors seek the safety and stability of government securities to escape from turmoil in international stock and bond markets. The resultant buying of government securities generally causes the credit spread to widen. A notable example of a flight-to-quality event occurred in 1998, when Russia defaulted on its debt.

Example

The one-year U.S. Treasury bill TED, trading at LIBOR minus 52.25 basis points on March 4, was an attractive trade for several reasons. First, the TED was trading at the lower end of the recent trading range, and, given comments made by the Federal Reserve, the likelihood that the supply of future one-year bills would be reduced was high. There was another compelling factor to consider: The old one-year bill was extremely special (a bond whose supply is

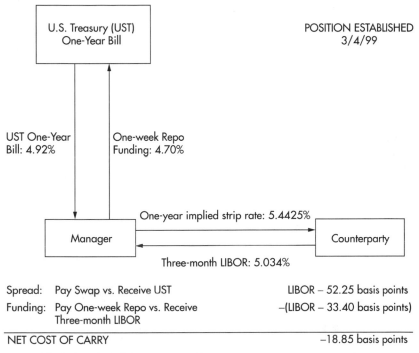

U.S. Treasury (UST) One-Year Bill		POSITION ESTABLISHED 3/4/99

UST One-Year Bill: 4.92%

One-week Repo Funding: 4.70%

One-year implied strip rate: 5.4425%

Manager

Counterparty

Three-month LIBOR: 5.034%

Spread:	Pay Swap vs. Receive UST	LIBOR − 52.25 basis points
Funding:	Pay One-week Repo vs. Receive Three-month LIBOR	−(LIBOR − 33.40 basis points)
NET COST OF CARRY		−18.85 basis points

Source: John Carlson, Springfield & Company LLC

tight is said to be "on special") in the financing market, and had remained so for some time. The probability of other traders' taking profits in the old one-year bill and rolling them into the new one-year bill also made the trade promising. The circumstances allowed the manager to be long the benchmark on-the-run (newly issued) bill without paying the benchmark "premium." (Newly issued benchmark Treasury securities usually trade at lower yields because they are considered more liquid than off-the-run, or old bonds, of the same maturity.) Over the previous few auction cycles, the typical premium for the current issue had been between three and 10 basis points. When the one-year TED widened to LIBOR minus 56.20 basis points in the next five days, the manager took profit on the position.

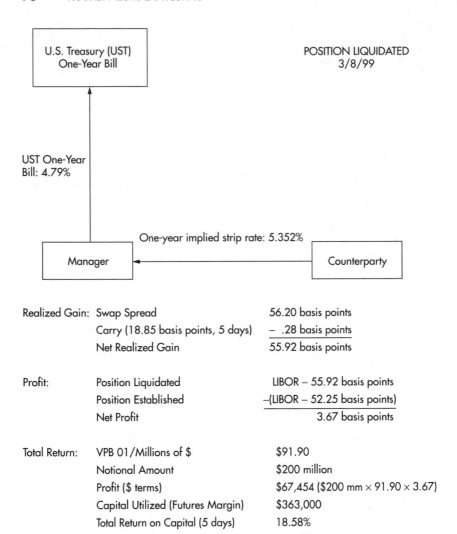

Realized Gain: Swap Spread .... 56.20 basis points
Carry (18.85 basis points, 5 days) .... – .28 basis points
Net Realized Gain .... 55.92 basis points

Profit: Position Liquidated .... LIBOR – 55.92 basis points
Position Established .... –(LIBOR – 52.25 basis points)
Net Profit .... 3.67 basis points

Total Return: VPB 01/Millions of $ $91.90
Notional Amount .... $200 million
Profit ($ terms) .... $67,454 ($200 mm × 91.90 × 3.67)
Capital Utilized (Futures Margin) ... $363,000
Total Return on Capital (5 days) ... 18.58%

Source: John Carlson, Springfield & Company LLC

Yield Curve Arbitrage

Yield curve arbitrage refers to an array of trades that involve taking long and short positions at different points on the U.S. Treasury yield curve in order to profit from relative pricing disparities.

Supply and demand for Treasury securities, as well as exogenous factors, such as central-bank policy actions, government issuance cycles, liquidity preference, and futures hedging, affect the shape and steepness of the yield curve. These factors may create anomalous kinks in the yield curve or spread differentials that represent profit opportunities for yield curve arbitrageurs.

The trades can be categorized by the maturities of the long and the short positions. Trades involving securities of very close maturities will usually be driven by structural or issuance cycle factors. Often, these issue-driven yield curve arbitrage trades make use of three securities (referred to as a butterfly) or more, over a short range of maturity. Issue-driven yield curve arbitrage trades seek to profit from "kinks" in the yield curve rather than from the steepness of the curve. By using multiple securities, managers can minimize the effect of changes in the slope of the yield curve on the trade. A classic example of an issuance-driven trade is "on-the-run" Treasury bonds versus "off-the-run" Treasury bonds. Newly issued 30-year Treasury bonds (on-the-run) will usually have lower yields than old 30-year Treasury bonds (off-the-run) because they are more liquid and often carry a premium in the financing market. A manager buys the off-the-run Treasury bond and sells the on-the-run Treasury bond with the expectation that, over time, the yields of the two bonds will eventually converge. If the expected convergence occurs, then the manager makes profits in proportion to the original spread between the two securities, less financing costs. The risk is that conditions can change dramatically and unexpectedly between the current and future dates (for example, a fundamental change can occur in the debt structure of the federal government). Alternatively, this trade can be initiated in the opposite direction, based on anomalies and changes in liquidity or financing conditions between the two issues.

At the other end of the yield curve arbitrage spectrum are trades in which the difference in the maturities of the two securities is larger. Thus, the relationship is often dependent on broader market factors (such as macroeconomic conditions) rather than being due to pure quantitative misalignment. A classic example is two-year notes versus 10-year notes. Many observers would classify these trades as relative value plays rather than yield curve arbitrage. But it is important to note here that there is a spectrum of yield curve arbitrage trades. The following example falls in the middle of the spectrum.

Example

As an example of a yield curve arbitrage trade, consider two off-the-run U.S. Treasuries, the 5¾ due 4/30/03 and the 6¼ due 2/28/02, in August 1998. According to statistical models, the four-year bond had become cheap relative to the five-year bond. As a background to this, Russia had defaulted on its debt, creating a flight from emerging market debt and other risky instruments to the safety of Treasury bonds. Investors' increased preference for liquidity created significant pressure at the short end of the U.S. Treasury curve and in current on-the-run issues, and gave the Fed good reason to consider lowering rates. In addition, the resulting "kink" in the two- to five-year segment of the yield curve provided an attractive "roll return" profile to the trade; that is, in a static market, the four-year issue was poised to age (or "roll") into a lower yielding segment of the curve, and the five-year issue was positioned to age into a higher yielding segment of the curve. Buying the off-the-run four-year note and selling the off-the-run five-year note allowed the manager room to benefit from the increasing liquidity preference (near the current five-year issue) without having to pay the financing premium associated with the current five-year note.

In this example, the manager's analysis of these events matched the statistical indications given by his models, so he entered the trade on August 21. The manager bought the four-year notes and sold short the five-year notes in proportion. The dollar value of a one-basis-point move in rates was then equal; in other words, the trade had zero parallel duration. Thus, the potential source of return was dependent on the spread between the two securities and the financing cost. The target exit spread was zero, and the financing market was such that the trade was put on with a small negative carry. Figure 5.1 shows the closing spread from July 3 through November 20.

The drastic change in the spread between the two securities coincided with the height of the liquidity crisis that culminated in the second Fed rate cut, on October 15. The global financial crisis served as a catalyst to correct (in this case, overcorrect, to the benefit of the manager) a relative misvaluation between two related

Figure 5.1   U.S. Treasury Historical Spread: 5¾ Due 04/30/03 vs. 6¼ Due 02/28/02*

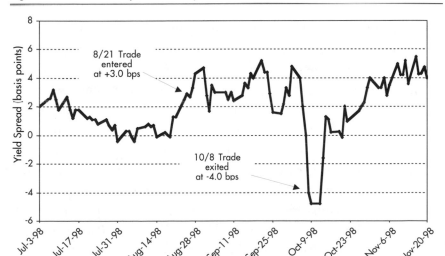

*Chart for indicative purposes only. Daily closing spreads based on Bloomberg's Generic pricing and actual intraday and executable spread levels may be significantly different.

securities. The manager exited the trade on October 8, having profited from the price effect of a seven-basis-point move in the relationship (the spread traded right through the target exit spread), less the cost of carrying the trade.

Relative Value Trades

Relative value trades, in the fixed-income realm, are trades in which the long and the short components are on different parts of the yield curve or in different fixed-income sectors, but their values are still linked in some manner. In almost all cases, no structural or technical factor in the fixed-income market can force a convergence of value. The opportunities are driven by relative misvaluations. Typically, the trade has a positive carry and a positively skewed distribution of expected returns. "Positively skewed" means that the expected returns are not evenly distributed around the average (in other words, in a bell curve); instead, more returns fall on the positive side.

Often, opportunities for relative value trades are the result of temporary credit anomalies, and the returns are derived from riding out the credit anomaly and obtaining advantageous financing. A manager might take a long position in a bond and short a swap at one point on the yield curve, and do the inverse at a different point on the curve. The relative pricing disparity between the two points is driven by investors' preference for securities offered at different points on the curve. An example of such an anomaly occurred in 1998 when the liquidation of Long Term Capital Management's positions produced a 40-basis-point difference between four- and five-year bonds in the United Kingdom (the historical range was closer to zero to 10 basis points). The manager who enters this kind of trade correctly takes profits when the credit anomaly works itself out.

In other cases, the relationship between the components is much more subjective. For example, a manager might go long in securities in the corporate sector and short in securities in the government sector, if he or she feels that the spread between the two will tighten. Because the relationship between the components is often somewhat subjective, in many relative value trades there is no way to force a convergence of value.

RISKS AND RISK CONTROL

Risks

Interest Rate or Market Risk

The value of almost all fixed-income instruments is influenced directly by interest rates (which can be thought of as the price of borrowing money). If interest rates drop, the prices of existing fixed-income securities will rise because their fixed coupon payments stay the same. The change in the price of the security reflects the increased value of that fixed stream of cash flows, given the lower levels of interest being offered currently. Interest rate changes, initiated by the central bank or otherwise, can realign the values of the entire fixed-income sector.

In the United States, monetary (more specifically, interest rate) policy is linked to the real economy. The central bank sets targets for two key short-term interest rates (the federal funds rate and the discount rate) and uses interest rate policy to promote growth or rein in inflation. The Fed tends to raise interest rates when it perceives inflationary pressures and to lower interest rates when the economy needs stimulation. Thus, fixed-income investors watch indicators of the real economy—the Consumer Price Index, the Producer Price Index, hourly earnings, the unemployment rate, gross domestic product, and retail sales—to try to determine how changes in wages, labor, output, and price levels will affect interest rates in the future.

Central bank policy is by no means the only factor affecting interest rates. Perceptions of happenings in the real economy, as well as perceptions of what future central bank policy will be, are as important as, if not more important than, the fundamental events themselves. Often, by the time the Fed raises or lowers interest rates, the rate change has already been factored into prices through investor perceptions. It is also important to note that the central bank does not have a monopoly on interest rates. Its interest rate policies reflect perceptions of the domestic economy and, increasingly, the global economy. The two rate cuts in the fall of 1998 (discussed later in this chapter) are excellent examples of how events that are exogenous to the U.S. real economy can set off, in U.S. financial markets, a liquidity crisis that threatens to disrupt the real economy, and thus, may prompt the Fed to inject liquidity into the system.

Credit Risk

The value of a fixed-income security is contingent upon the credit quality of the issuer—in other words, the issuer's ability to continue to repay interest and principal. A security issued by a company that defaults on its debt becomes almost worthless.

Fixed-income securities in the United States are rated by two major rating agencies: Standard & Poor's and Moody's. The ratings of these two agencies provide a guide to the credit quality of issuing entities. In addition, managers can compare the credit quality of a particular issuer with that of similar issuers. For example, the debt of an energy company that is rated B has a higher coupon than the bonds of the companies in its peer group that are rated BBB-. Even though the entities are similar, the B security pays a higher coupon and thus may represent a good value relative to its peer group. Managers may try to avoid credit quality exposure by being long and short equal amounts of similar credit quality issues.

Residual Currency Exposure

In trades that involve securities denominated in foreign currencies, a manager must hedge the trade back into domestic currency in order to avoid unwanted currency bets on top of the fixed-income trade. This is done using currency futures contracts. In practice, currency hedges are not always perfect; thus, residual currency exposure is a risk.

Counterparty Risk

Most fixed-income arbitrage trades involve both borrowing and lending (going long and short), so the manager must be both borrower and lender. The relationship with other entities, either as a borrower or a lender of securities, is called a counterparty relationship. By entering into such a relationship, the manager runs the risk that the counterparty will, in effect, default on its end of an arrangement. This possibility requires managers to research the creditworthiness of counterparties before entering into relationships with them. Counterparty risk generally reveals itself in crisis situations, as evidenced in the fall of 1998. Since that time, dealers and managers alike are doing a great deal more due diligence on their counterparties, to ensure their creditworthiness.

Model Risk

Many fixed-income arbitrage managers depend heavily on quantitative models to identify pricing anomalies in fixed-income markets. For these managers to be successful, their quantitative models must accurately predict pricing relationships. There is always the risk that a model that has exhibited predictive value in the past will fail to do so in the future. Thus, the use of quantitative models requires constant vigilance and reassessment, to ensure their predictive accuracy.

Tail Risk

Even when quantitative models work, they usually identify opportunities within a 95 percent confidence interval. Managers, therefore, must be wary of the other 5 percent. Ninety-five percent accuracy may imply that a particular occurrence will happen only once in a lifetime, but there is no clue for *when* in that lifetime. Just such a "multiple standard deviation" occurrence caused the Long Term Capital Management debacle (discussed later in this chapter).

Government Policy Risk

As previously mentioned, the role of the central bank in changing or not changing interest rates is a risk factor. Other government policy moves, such as changes in tax laws or issuance of new Treasury securities, can have equally significant effects on the value of fixed-income securities. To control these risks, managers must be aware of political as well as financial happenings.

Liquidity Risk

As with any asset class, managers must pay a premium for the most liquid fixed-income securities. If they choose to hold less liquid securities, they will usually receive a higher yield than if they hold more liquid securities, but they run the risk of having in their portfolio a security that they cannot sell whenever they choose. In a normal market scenario, some of the liquidity premium is embedded in the bid–ask spreads for different securities. Furthermore, in a stress period, the value of illiquid securities can drop, on a mark-to-market basis, especially in a flight-to-quality situation.

In addition, the liquidity of a particular instrument can change as the overall demand for liquidity in the market changes. Thus, in the liquidity squeeze during August and September 1998, corporate bonds that were normally judged to be very liquid became increasingly less so, particularly when compared with the liquidity provided by Treasuries. Managers must be aware of and control implicit liquidity bets embedded in seemingly innocuous spread trades.

Measuring and Controlling Interest Rate Risk

Duration

Fixed-income arbitrageurs insulate themselves from market risk by taking offsetting long and short positions in similar securities whose values are historically or statistically interrelated. "Statistically interrelated" most often refers to duration.

Duration is a measure of how sensitive a bond's price is to a shift in interest rates. For example, if a bond has a duration of two years, then the bond's value will decline approximately 2 percent for each 1 percent increase in interest rates, or rise approximately 2 percent for each 1 percent fall in interest rates. Such a bond is less interest-rate-sensitive than a bond of similar credit quality with a five-year duration, which will decline in value approximately 5 percent for each 1 percent increase in interest rates, and rise approximately 5 percent for each 1 percent decrease. Roughly,

$$\text{Duration} = \frac{\text{Change in price} / \text{Price}}{\text{Change in interest rates}}.$$

Duration is equal to the average maturity of bonds for which a particular price–yield relationship holds. Bonds with longer maturities will be more affected by a change in interest rates because that change will be felt over a longer period of time. For example, an investor buys a five-year bond with a coupon rate of 6 percent, and a 10-year bond of similar credit quality with a similar rate of 6 percent. Subsequently, interest rates rise 1 percent. Both bonds are now less attractive than when they were bought, because the investor could now get the same interest rate for less money. The price of the five-year bond, however, reflects the present value of its now less favorable rate over only five years, whereas the 10-year bond reflects the present value of its rate over 10 years. Accordingly, the price of the bond with a longer maturity will be more sensitive to changes in interest rates than the bond with the shorter maturity.

Fixed-income arbitrageurs buy one bond and sell short another bond with similar duration. If interest rates change, the effect, in dollar terms, on the long position will be offset by the short position because both bonds respond the same way to the change. If the total duration of the long side of a portfolio is equal to the total duration of the short side, the portfolio is said to have zero duration. Fixed-income arbitrageurs try to eliminate market risk by structuring their trades and portfolios to be at or near zero duration. Any foreign currency risk is hedged against in a similar fashion, using currency futures contracts.

Parallel and Rotational Shifts of the Yield Curve

Fixed-income arbitrage managers often attempt to insulate their portfolios from both parallel and rotational shifts in the yield curve. Parallel duration calculations estimate the sensitivity of the price of the portfolio with respect to different magnitudes of parallel shifts of the yield curve. Rotational duration calculations estimate the sensitivity of the price of the portfolio to yield-curve pivots of various magnitudes (a pivot is achieved by holding one point on the curve constant while changing another). The pivot points are usually bellwether points such as the three-month yield and the 10-year yield.

SOURCES OF RETURN

Although few pure arbitrages still exist, fixed-income arbitrage strategies have a nondirectional philosophical orientation that qualifies them to be included in discussions of market-neutral strategies. Fixed-income arbitrageurs make bets on *the relationship between two or more securities*, rather than on market direction. They construct trades involving securities whose relationship is temporarily out of sync. In some cases, managers construct a "synthetic option" (as in a basis trade) that allows them to buy the potential upside at a limited and defined cost that represents the worst-case scenario.

In normal market environments, fixed-income arbitrage shows very little correlation to general market indexes, indicating that returns are derived from other sources. Nevertheless, as with many investment strategies, in serious downturns, many relationships that have held historically can become dislocated in a way that works against fixed-income arbitrageurs. Thus, the relationship between securities is not necessarily a more stable source of return than the market, but it is certainly a different and nondirectional one.

In a normal market environment, fixed-income arbitrage returns are based on the relationship between two or more fixed income securities rather than on the direction of the fixed-income markets. Fixed-income arbitrage returns, therefore, are not strongly correlated to overall fixed-income market movement under most market conditions. As discussed later in this chapter, this statement is less true in periods of extreme market movements. Generally, fixed-income arbitrage specialists can achieve ample and stable returns over time by evaluating and selecting undervalued fixed-income securities and hedging them with related securities, as opposed to submitting to the far more random nature of most directional investment strategies.

This chapter has touched on some of the sources of return for particular kinds of fixed-income arbitrage trades, but some more general categories apply across all of the trades.

Financing

Because most fixed-income strategies take the form of spread trades in which the spread is not particularly large, the trades must be leveraged—often, many times—to produce a competitive return. Therefore, fixed-income arbitrage managers must be able to obtain attractive financing. To establish the credit lines and counterparty relationships that fixed-income arbitrage strategies require, a manager must have a relatively large minimum amount of capital under management (generally, $25 to $50 million).

Repurchase Agreements

A repurchase agreement, or Repo, refers to the financing of specific bonds long or short. Fluctuations in supply and demand for a particular bond can cause the market for financing a position in that bond to vary widely. A bond whose supply is tight is said to be "on special." A short seller of such a bond will receive less than market rates on the short proceeds, so any arbitrage involving that bond is less profitable. The ability to get good Repo quotes is a driving factor behind many arbitrages.

Technology

Fixed-income managers sometimes refer to "complexity premiums." These are the costs of the complex quantitative modeling and large amount of computer modeling needed to analyze fixed-income securities. Many managers feel that they are paid to understand relationships that others don't, but this level of understanding often becomes a matter of technology. Some managers spend hundreds of thousands of dollars on computer systems that can analyze and manage a fixed-income portfolio. Some of the returns, therefore, are attributable to the investment in technology. However, technology has become a factor that is necessary but not sufficient to ensure success. Technology can bring better data to the manager faster and make it easier to analyze, but the analysis is still the manager's realm.

Liquidity

More liquid securities command a premium over less liquid but similar securities. Thus, managers who are willing to hold less liquid securities may derive some of their profit from "capturing" the liquidity premium. They hold the less liquid security and simultaneously sell the more liquid security short, but they run the risk of getting stuck with a security for which, at any given time, there are few buyers. Managers should be aware of their overall exposure to liquidity in their portfolio. For example, a manager could have a portfolio of trades that is diversified in all other aspects, but the short positions are all in less liquid securities. In a liquidity squeeze, this exposure would override all other factors.

Events

Some fixed-income arbitrages result from extraordinary market events or from the perceived possibility of a forthcoming event. Fixed-income arbitrageurs may invest in these situations in a hedged fashion, to profit from a perceived or actual credit anomaly created by the event. An example of such an event would be a perceived risk of tax law changes.

Manager Skill and Hard Work

Fixed-income arbitrage involves a great deal of sifting through data to find arbitrage or arbitrage-like situations. As fixed-income markets become more and more efficient, arbitrage-like opportunities become fewer and harder to find. In addition, the number of managers chasing these arbitrage profits can narrow the spreads. With the downfall of Long Term Capital Management and the scaling-back of other large players during the third and fourth quarters of 1998, the field was thinned. Managers who have been able to survive have exhibited a good measure of skill and hard work.

GROWTH AND RECENT DEVELOPMENTS IN FIXED-INCOME ARBITRAGE

Fixed-income arbitrage as a hedge fund strategy tripled from 0.6 percent of hedge fund assets in 1990 to about 1.8 percent in 1999. This increase masks the negative returns and pullback that occurred in the second half of 1998. In addition, many relative value arbitrage and mortgage-backed securities managers are engaged in forms of fixed-income arbitrage. Thus, the above figure probably understates the amount of assets in the strategy.

The third and fourth quarters of 1998 were disastrous for many fixed-income arbitrageurs. The managers included in the HFRI Fixed-Income Arbitrage Index averaged –6.45 percent returns in September, –6.09 percent in October, and –10.29 percent for the year. These numbers include only a subset of hedge fund managers who employed the strategy, and may mask even more damage done to the proprietary desks of major brokerage houses and cross-arbitrage players. During the period, relative valuations moved into territory never before seen, confounding the underlying logic of all manner of traditional arbitrage plays. Trades that benefited from the overriding flight-to-quality—mainly, TED spreads—were the exception. In any case, during this period, the strategy fared as badly as, or perhaps worse than, any of the other market-neutral strategies. What is important is why this downturn occurred.

Many fixed-income arbitrage players refer to the events of August, September, and October 1998 as "multiple standard deviation" events. This phrase refers to events that were possible but were highly unlikely to occur, considering the normal distribution that underlies most quantitative models. Many events that happened during this period had never occurred before, and statistical models had predicted, with 95 percent confidence, that they would not occur. In other words, the distortion of spread relationships that occurred in fixed-income markets was highly unusual—but not impossible.

Coming into August, there was an overextension of capital in fixed-income arbitrage. More participants and more money than ever were involved in those trades, which resulted in tighter arbitrage spreads. To extract the excess returns they had come to expect, participants used more leverage than normal. All of these factors created a precarious situation that went sour when Russia defaulted on $40 billion of internal debt and delivered an overriding liquidity squeeze in global financial markets. All manner of credit spreads blew out to historical highs.

During the crisis, a large number of fixed-income trades that were not historically correlated became so. Thus, the following trades—which, on their face, seem unrelated—acted very similarly: Russian debt versus G-10 debt; corporate debt versus government debt; off-the-run Treasuries versus on-the-run Treasuries; Canadian government bonds versus U.S. Treasury bonds; mortgage-backed securities versus Treasuries; and illiquid mortgage-backed securities versus liquid mortgage-backed securities. In each case, the manager would have gotten stuck on the wrong side of quality. This is an example of how correlations that are stable in the long run can become highly unstable in the short term. The inherent short-term instability of correlations is very difficult to model, and many managers do not incorporate it into their quantitative models. Model risk became all too apparent as the overriding liquidity squeeze caused correlations to converge.

During this time, rapid and unusual changes took place in the term structure of interest rates for U.S. Treasuries. As Figure 5.2 illustrates, by September 10, the term structure of U.S. interest rates had changed dramatically. Notably, the yield on all Treasuries, which has an inverse relationship to price, had dropped significantly, which was to be expected as global financial instability led investors to move money into safe Treasury bonds. In addition, the curve had steepened as demand for the short end outstripped demand for the long end. But perhaps more important, while the longer maturity issues (10-year and 30-year) had gone through a parallel shift, the short end of the curve had become inverted. The

Figure 5.2 U.S. Treasury Yield Curves: Q3 Inversion

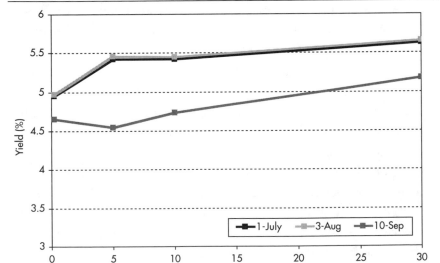

yield on the 90-day bill exceeded that on the five-year bill. Popular wisdom has it that an inverted yield curve anticipates a recession. Needless to say, this development in the fixed-income market did nothing to dispel mounting worries about global recession.

As Figure 5.3 shows, the term structure of interest rates displayed further radical changes between early September and the second Fed rate cut (October 16). From mid-September through the first cut (October 1), yields on all maturities had fallen in parallel, retaining the inverted character of the curve as a whole. Following the rate cut, demand for the shorter maturities shot up, and the curve pivoted, returning to a more normal (by historical standards) shape. But the fixed-income markets continued to exhibit structural disturbances through the new year, as liquidity returned.

In addition, the overriding liquidity preference distorted normal fixed-income spread relationships. Figure 5.4 shows the daily yields for Treasury securities of different maturities.

Figure 5.3 U.S. Treasury Yield Curves: 9/10, 10/1, 10/16

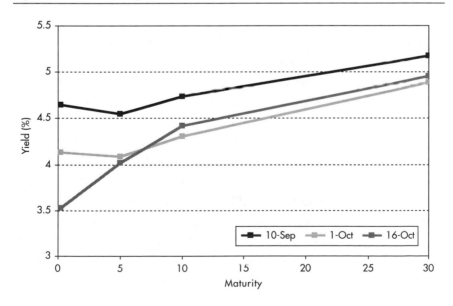

Figure 5.4 U.S. Treasury Securities Yield

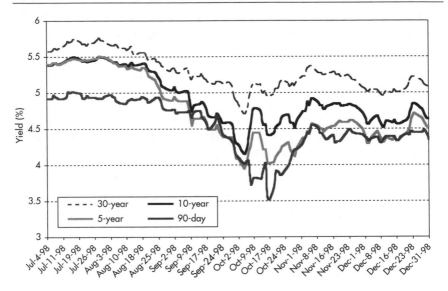

The problem was exacerbated by a confluence of positions in the portfolios of large hedge funds and the proprietary desks of major Wall Street brokerage houses. Dealers who were required to protect collateral did not have sufficient equity to meet market demand. Thus, they were left with two options: (1) take a directional position, or (2) liquidate the long exposure. The latter option was behind the bailout of Long Term Capital Management (LTCM), the largest hedge fund using fixed-income arbitrage, by a Wall Street consortium that included Morgan Stanley, Merrill Lynch, Salomon Smith Barney, and Goldman Sachs. Coming into August, LTCM had a huge portfolio of highly leveraged fixed-income arbitrage trades. By injecting liquidity into the fixed-income markets, the bailout helped save major Street arbitrage players who shared positions with LTCM from potential losses by allowing for an organized and orderly liquidation of LTCM's fixed-income arbitrage portfolio.

In early August, the amount of leverage used by fixed-income arbitrageurs made the stability of creditors a major issue. When the Street made margin calls in an effort to rein in risk exposure, even funds with well-articulated models and lower levels of leverage had to be afraid that their credit lines could be pulled at any time. Managers reduced the risk profiles of their portfolios by de-leveraging— dumping still more product on the market. Leverage concerns increased in early October as brokerages cut credit to Ellington Capital, a major mortgage-backed securities fund, and other money management operations. The crisis peaked on October 9 with massive uncertainty about whether LTCM and the proprietary desks would continue to liquidate positions, and whether the Street would continue to cut financing. Soon after, the Federal Reserve lowered interest rates twice within a two-week period, injecting liquidity into the markets and providing a measure of relief.

The aftermath of the 1998 crisis brought major changes in the landscape of the fixed-income arbitrage world. There were, suddenly, fewer players, and less money was chasing arbitrage spreads. Spreads have become more volatile, and dislocations tend to last longer. The risk premium paid to participants has gone up—in step with the Street's reduced appetite and capacity to take on risk. Opportunities were created for managers who are willing and able to step in as intermediaries and provide liquidity to the market. The Street has become more diligent about researching counterparties and extending credit lines. As a consequence, large and highly leveraged transactions at tight spreads are both difficult to come by and difficult to execute. In spite of negative performance by the fixed-income markets as a whole, the performance of managers in the HFRI Fixed-Income Arbitrage Index in 1999 returned to a level commensurate with their historical average. Historical returns for the strategy are shown in Table 5.1. The growth of $1,000 invested in fixed-income arbitrage (as measured by the HFRI Fixed-Income Arbitrage Index) is illustrated in Figure 5.5.

Table 5.1   Returns from Fixed-Income Arbitraged Investments, 1990–1999

Number of Funds	Average Size (Millions of $US)	Year	Jan	Feb	Mar	Apr	May
4	35	1990	2.25	2.10	−0.21	2.23	0.32
4	37	1991	4.00	2.42	1.52	1.88	2.34
5	43	1992	4.70	2.53	2.53	2.26	0.62
9	56	1993	0.25	0.89	1.47	1.45	1.94
13	97	1994	2.32	1.63	0.93	0.98	0.75
21	99	1995	0.64	0.34	1.79	0.64	−0.54
24	115	1996	0.95	0.69	0.58	1.39	1.15
23	130	1997	1.43	1.17	0.54	0.98	0.34
25	203	1998	0.39	1.28	1.34	1.03	0.19
23	103	1999	1.17	1.09	1.31	0.11	−0.03

Annual represents geometric compounded average.

Figure 5.5   Fixed-Income Arbitrage: Growth of $1,000, January 1990–December 1999

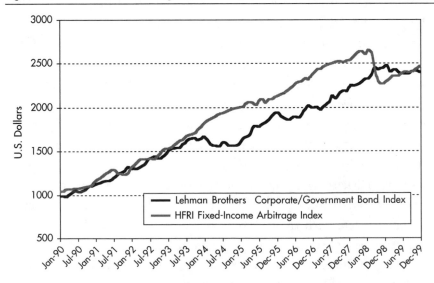

Jun	Jul	Aug	Sep	Oct	Nov	Dec	Annual*
0.15	0.68	0.03	0.49	1.22	0.55	0.57	10.84
1.39	1.96	−0.82	−2.58	−0.03	−1.17	1.46	12.89
−0.45	−0.08	0.84	−0.79	3.33	2.18	2.62	22.11
0.37	1.99	1.50	0.70	0.96	2.12	1.87	16.64
1.32	0.36	0.71	0.88	0.65	0.76	0.06	11.94
−1.18	2.49	0.92	−1.89	1.58	0.01	1.22	6.08
1.35	1.30	0.63	0.52	1.18	−0.37	1.94	11.89
0.67	0.58	0.40	0.51	−0.37	−0.14	0.71	6.87
−1.31	1.69	−1.18	−6.45	−6.09	−1.42	0.15	−10.29
1.32	0.65	−0.34	0.39	0.51	1.18	1.19	8.87

Mortgage-Backed Securities Arbitrage

6

Mortgage-backed securities arbitrage is a particular kind of fixed-income arbitrage. More specifically, it can be referred to as a type of fixed-income relative value trading (discussed in Chapter 5).

A mortgage-backed security (MBS) represents an ownership interest in mortgage loans made by financial institutions—such as savings and loans, commercial banks, or mortgage companies—to finance borrowers' purchases of homes. From an investor's standpoint, an MBS is a fixed-income security with underlying prepayment options. MBS arbitrage managers use proprietary models to value and rank the embedded options of MBSs, and, ultimately, to rank the securities by option-adjusted spreads (OAS). Considering the prepayment options, an MBS arbitrage manager calculates a present value of the security's future cash flows—in other words, an option-adjusted price. By using the option-adjusted price rather than the security's current market price, the option-adjusted spread reflects the security's average spread over Treasury securities of similar maturity. The OAS can be interpreted as the security's incremental return over Treasuries, adjusted for the effects of interest rate volatility and its impact on the MBS's prepayment tendencies.

The securities that offer the best value are bought and hedged to zero duration using Treasuries, Treasury options, futures, caps, floors, swaps, and forward contracts. By maintaining zero duration, managers avoid making unwanted bets on the direction of interest rates and can concentrate on deriving returns from security valuation and selection. Mortgage managers can be distinguished by what sector of the MBS market they invest in (there are many different kinds of MBS structures with customized risk-and-return characteristics), the valuation systems they use, and their risk management or hedging practices.

MORTGAGE-BACKED STRUCTURES OR SECTORS (TYPES OF MBS INSTRUMENTS)

To distinguish among MBS managers and understand their strategies, one must understand the complex world of mortgage-backed securities. This chapter discusses the different kinds of mortgage-backed instruments that have evolved over time, and the risk-and-return profiles that these securities have offered. A defining feature of a manager's strategy is what sector (or sectors) of the MBS market is chosen for investment. Some managers restrict themselves to particular sectors because of liquidity and risk considerations; others invest in the sectors that they believe offer the best relative value.

Mortgage-Backed Securities' Evolution

As noted earlier in this chapter, a mortgage-backed security represents a financial institution's ownership interest in a mortgage loan that is made to finance a borrower's purchase of a home. Government agencies such as the Government National Mortgage Association (GNMA or "Ginnie Mae"), government-sponsored enterprises such as the Federal National Mortgage Association (FNMA or "Fannie Mae"), and some other financial entities, pool mortgage loans in a trust and issue securities that represent a direct ownership in that trust. Table 6.1 lists the major issuing entities, their nicknames, and the type of institution they are.

The practice of pooling mortgages and issuing securities on them is relatively new. In 1978, Bob Dall, a Salomon Brothers trader, together with Stephen Joseph, created the first private issue of mortgage securities. In the deal, Bank of America sold, in the form of bonds, home loans it had made to institutional investors. Bank of America received cash for the bonds, which it could then

Table 6.1   The Major U.S. Mortgage Issuers

Agency	Nickname	Structure
Government National Mortgage Association (GNMA)	Ginnie Mae	Government-owned corporation Department of Housing and Urban Development (HUD)
Federal National Mortgage Association (FNMA)	Fannie Mae	Government-sponsored corporation
Federal Home Loan Mortgage Corporation (FHLMC)	Freddie Mac	Government-sponsored corporation

relend, and the original mortgage payments *passed through* to the holders of the bonds. The niche did not really take off until the fall of 1981, when Congress passed a tax break that gave thrifts an incentive to sell their mortgage loans. The only fully staffed mortgage bond trading desk on Wall Street at the time, Salomon Brothers, became a hugely profitable enterprise, and a new market emerged.[1] Over time, mortgage securities have evolved from the original pass-throughs to more complicated structures with customized risk-and-reward characteristics.

Like traditional bonds, MBSs have an interest component and a principal component. Unlike traditional bonds, many MBSs have uncertain maturity dates because every mortgagee in the pool has the option to refinance or prepay the mortgage. Like the prices of traditional bonds, MBS prices fluctuate in response to interest rates. But interest rates have an additional effect on MBSs. Generally, when interest rates decline, prepayments accelerate beyond the initial pricing assumptions, which causes the average life and expected maturity of the MBS to shorten. On the other hand,

---

[1] For a discussion of Salomon Brothers' role in the development of the mortgage-back bond market, see Michael Lewis, *Liar's Poker* (New York: 1989), pp. 79–151.

when interest rates rise, prepayments slow down beyond the initial pricing assumptions and can cause the average life and expected maturity of the MBS to increase. When prepayments increase because of a drop in interest rates, the principal of the security may have to be invested at a lower interest rate than the coupon of the security.

Although prepayments are a function of interest rates, they do not have a one-to-one relationship with new rates. Changes in the level of prepayments are caused by one of four things: death, disaster, relocation, or refinancing. Only the latter is directly linked to interest rates. Thus, prepayment risk can be difficult to quantify. Because the borrower has the option to prepay the mortgage, MBSs contain an embedded option. The price that an investor must be paid to accept this option increases as the propensity to refinance increases. These securities, however, are often mispriced because it is so difficult to exactly predict prepayments. Generally, MBSs have higher yields than traditional bonds because of prepayment risk.

Although MBSs may seem very different from traditional fixed-income instruments, fixed-income investors are looking for the same things in both. At the end of the day, investors must judge whether the reward that an instrument offers (coupon), given the price at which it is being offered (price of the security), is worth the risk (credit risk, market risk, or prepayment risk) associated with that instrument. When the market over- or under-values a security, an opportunity for relative value arbitrage profits exists.

The evolution of the MBS market has been driven by investors' demand for customized risk and cash flows. Dealers and issuing agencies have been allowed to strip mortgage pools into different tranches of securities with different risk-and-reward characteristics. This chapter describes some of the more common MBS structures. To understand the different kinds of structures, it is important to remember that, over time, dealers created new investment options when demand was such that the sum of the component parts [i.e., collateralized mortgage obligation (CMO) tranches] could be sold to investors for a higher amount than the cost of purchasing the underlying collateral (i.e., the original mortgage pool or pass-throughs). By engineering customized securities, CMO originators simultaneously increase the number of possible MBS investors and create an arbitrage for themselves. They continue to do so today; however, some of the structures described in this chapter may not be available because it may not be profitable for originators to create them at the current time.

Throughout the late 1970s and into the early 1980s, almost all MBS securities were of the most basic ilk: pass-throughs, or simply a participation in the cash flows produced by pooled mortgages. In 1983, an unusually large drop in mortgage rates and a powerful housing market allowed almost double the number of mortgages to be originated. That same year, the FHLMC (Freddie Mac) created a new class of security: the collateralized mortgage obligation (CMO). The original CMO stripped the cash flows from a pool of mortgages and created short, intermediate, and long-term tranches. As demand increased over time, more and more specialized securities were created to meet investors' demands.

Pass-Throughs

Pass-throughs are securities that allow investors to participate in cash flows produced by pooled mortgage loans made on single-family residences. To ensure that issuing the securities will be profitable for them, the issuing entities offer a coupon on pass-through securities that is 50 to 75 basis points less than the rate the homeowner pays them. The difference is the cost to the agency for issuing the security, and it includes servicing, trustee expenses, and an agency guarantee.

Most U.S. pass-throughs are issued by the government or by the government-sponsored agencies listed previously: Ginnie Mae, Fannie Mae, and Freddie Mac. Standard mortgage pass-throughs have a 30-year term, a fixed coupon rate, and 360 monthly payments, and are prepayable at any time without a penalty. Thus, pass-throughs generally have long maturities and the potential for early repayment of principal. The cash flows generated by a pool of mortgages, and thus the maturity of a pass-through security, can vary dramatically, depending on the rate of prepayments.

Basic Collateralized Mortgage Obligations (CMOs)

CMOs add another layer to the MBS structure. They are created by pooling pools of mortgage collateral. Thus, pass-through securities may become collateral for a CMO. (In 1997, about 70 percent of pass-through securities were pledged as collateral for CMOs.) CMOs were created to combat the uncertain nature of the cash flows offered by pass-through securities. Different investors are interested in investments that have different durations and performance characteristics. For example, banks are interested in different kinds of securities than are endowments. CMO structures allow an issuer to carve up large pools of mortgage cash flows into classes and tranches customized to its investors' preferences. Factors that affect the profitability of issuing CMOs include: cost of collateral, demand for different classes of cash flows, CMO spreads (between CMOs and Treasuries), and the shape of the yield curve.

Sequential-Pay CMOs

Sequential-pay CMOs are broken down into classes that have differing average lives. The payment schedule is as follows:

1. *Interest* is paid to all classes, based on the principal amount outstanding at the beginning of the period.

2. *Principal and prepayments* are used to pay off the first class. All of the principal is directed to the first class until its principal share is reduced to zero.

3. All principal and prepayments are then directed to the second class, and so on, until each of the classes is paid off.

Sequential Pay with a Z Class

Z classes are used to push a deal's cash flow to the earlier classes and thus shorten their average life. The Z class pays no interest until all of the other classes are paid off. The Z class's principal factor will increase monthly by the amount of the interest deferred. The cash not paid to the Z class speeds up the payment of the earlier classes.

Sequential Pay with a Z Class and VADMs

Because Z class issuers know the exact amount of cash flow resulting from deferring interest from the Z bond, they can create a class of stable and predictable bonds. These securities, called VADMs (Very Accurately Defined Maturity Bonds), are also issued in sequential classes. The earlier classes are highly certain, and the longer classes are more subject to volatility, depending on the rate of prepayments.

PAC (Planned Amortization Class) Bonds

PAC bonds are sequential classes that use support bonds to offer a fixed principal schedule that can endure over a range of prepayment scenarios. Issuers determine the deal's likely maximum and minimum prepayment rates, thereby creating a *PAC band*. The role of the support bonds in the structure is to create stable cash flows so that the PAC bond's cash flow is unaltered, even when changes occur in the prepayment rate. Support bonds absorb prepayments when prepayments are higher than expected, and they defer principal payments when prepayments are slower than expected. Among the factors that affect the valuation of PAC bonds are:

- The width of the PAC band. In general, the wider the PAC band, the more stable the cash flows provided by the PAC bond, because the cash flows will be unaffected by a wider range of prepayment scenarios.

- The number of support bonds. The fewer support bonds in a deal, the less stable the PAC bonds will be, because support bonds serve as stabilizers.

- The type of collateral. PAC bonds and PAC bands should be considered in relation to the deal's underlying collateral. Specific kinds of collateral, such as seasoned collateral, are more likely to exhibit predictable prepayments than unseasoned collateral.

- The length (maturity) of PAC bonds. Compared to longer classes, shorter PAC bonds have more support bonds actively stabilizing cash flows during their lifetime. When all the support bonds have been retired, a PAC deal pays off in the same manner as a sequential-pay CMO. Thus, in the worst case, a buyer of a long PAC bond pays a premium for what essentially becomes a sequential-pay bond.

Support Bonds

Because support bonds act as shock absorbers for PAC bonds, they can show huge average life volatility when the rate of prepayments increases or decreases. Volatility is lower for support bonds that are less subject to prepayment risk. Factors influencing volatility include:

- The percentage of support bonds in the deal. The higher the percentage of support bonds to PAC bonds, the more diluted the effect of prepayment increases or decreases.
- Collateral. Specific kinds of collateral, such as seasoned collateral, are more likely to exhibit predictable prepayments than unseasoned collateral. In addition, discount collateral is less likely to experience prepayments.

Because support bonds can be highly volatile, the cash flows are often further stripped down or restructured to offer more attractive investment options.

CMO Tranches

Most CMO cash flows start as sequential-pays, PAC bonds, or support bonds. But, in a continuing effort to customize cash flows, issuers have created a number of ways to further carve up these cash flows into CMO tranches. The possibilities discussed here include: discount bonds, principal-only (PO) and interest-only (IO) strips, and floater/inverse floater combinations.

Coupon-Shifting Tranches

Coupon-shifting tranches are created when dealers can form two classes of cash flows—one at a premium to the original cash flows, and the other at a discount—and receive a higher price for the sum of the two classes than they would for the original structure. Coupon-shifting tranches are usually driven by customer requests that dictate how the original bond tranche is to be carved up.

POs and IOs

A single cash flow can be stripped down into a principal-only (PO) component that is not entitled to any interest income, and an interest-only (IO) component that does not have any real principal allocated to it. (The principal that produces the interest due on these bonds is the same principal cash flow used to pay down the PO. For the purposes of the IO strip, the principal is referred to as notional.)

Home mortgages generate three types of cash flow:

1. Regular interest payments, which tend to be heavily weighted in earlier periods, are allocated in full to the IO class.
2. Scheduled principal payments, which tend to increase as the loan ages, are allocated in full to the PO class.
3. Unscheduled prepayments, which may occur at any time, are allocated in full to the PO class.

If no prepayments occur, the vast majority of the cash flows in earlier periods are directed to the IO class. This situation would not reverse itself until late in the loan, when the interest due is nearly exhausted. However, if prepayments occur at, for example, a constant 20 percent rate, then the majority of cash flows throughout the life of the loan are directed to the PO class. Prepayments come completely at the expense of the IO class. The PO class receives the same total amount of cash in both scenarios, but the timing is different. (The cash flows are weighted toward earlier periods in the second scenario.) IO cash flows are extremely uncertain and contain an implicit bet about the timing and magnitude of prepayments. On the other hand, total PO cash flows are known, but their timing is not.

PAC IOs

As discussed in a previous section, PAC bonds are sequential classes that use support bonds to offer a fixed principal schedule that can hold over a range of prepayment scenarios. PAC IOs can be created from PAC bonds that are not full-coupon bonds. The result is a tranche of sequentially paid IO bonds. These tranches are typically front-loaded and vulnerable to prepayments. Like all IO cash flows, PAC IO cash flows are extremely uncertain and contain an implicit bet about the timing and magnitude of prepayments. However, it should be noted that PAC IOs are somewhat less risky than other IOs because they are based on PAC bonds that use support bonds to mitigate the prepayment risk. On the other hand, they usually offer a lower base case yield than other IO strips.

Floaters and Inverse Floaters

Dealers have created floating-rate assets to cater to a strong demand for assets that are a good match for liabilities based on short-term interest rates. Because the underlying MBS structures are fixed-rate assets, dealers strip them down into combinations of floaters and inverse floaters. Dealers are willing to do so because floaters are usually indexed to LIBOR (London Inter-Bank Offering Rate) and can typically be sold for more than the underlying collateral. The floater is usually sold at LIBOR plus some number of basis points, with a cap. The corresponding inverse floater has a floor below which it cannot drop. Inverse floaters with nonzero floors require less leverage than those with zero floors. However, the floor is often set at zero. The coupon for the inverse floater is determined by a formula that takes into account the amount of principal allocated to the inverse class, the amount of leverage applied to that principal, the floater cap, and LIBOR. The formulas are such that, under any possible scenario, the total aggregate coupon payment is equal to the coupon of the underlying collateral.

Unlike IO products, floaters and inverse floaters receive full principal balances. Coupon payments are less certain and more volatile, particularly in the leveraged inverse floater classes.

Two-Tiered Index Bonds (TTIBs)

TTIBs are created from the cash flows of an inverse floater. Dealers create TTIBs because they raise the caps of their related floaters and allow inverse floaters to be more highly leveraged and to be sold at deeper discounts. Because these features are attractive to investors, dealers can sell the new structure for more than the original floater/inverse floater structure.

TTIBs combine features of high-coupon fixed-rate bonds and inverse floaters. Over a range of interest rate index scenarios, TTIBs are fixed-rate bonds. The range is determined by its lower strike price, or first tier. The TTIB maintains its high fixed coupon unless LIBOR moves above the preset lower strike price. Above the strike price, the coupon is determined by an inverse floater-like equation that reduces the coupon as LIBOR rises. The complicated formula takes into account the total principal, the floater principal, the inverse principal, the TTIB principal, the TTIB leverage, the inverse leverage, the floater margin, the floater cap, and the strike price. The TTIB hits its second tier when the coupon becomes zero. The LIBOR rate at which this occurs is referred to as the bond's LIBOR cap.

Inverse IOs

Inverse IOs are created from fixed-rate bonds using a multiple-step process. First, the fixed-rate bond has to be stripped into a discount bond and a premium bond. The premium class is then subdivided into a floater class and an inverse IO class. The inverse IOs' coupon is equal to the difference between the fixed-rate coupon and the floater coupon. Because this coupon can be quite low, inverse IOs tend to be highly leveraged. In addition, inverse IOs receive no principal payments and are thus extremely sensitive to prepayments.

Valuation Methods

The primary tool MBS managers have at their disposal is asset selection. Because of the complex nature of MBS structures, this process is usually dependent on complex, computer-driven, quantitative valuation models. The two components in this process are the valuation model itself and the computing power and technology necessary to run the model.

Option-Adjusted Spreads

Most MBS managers' valuation models incorporate prepayment assumptions and evaluate interest-rate scenarios, to produce an option-adjusted spread (OAS). An OAS (1) represents the security's yield above the Treasury yield after accounting for the embedded prepayment option, and (2) is a manager's most useful tool for ranking securities and determining which ones offer the best relative values. However, to say that most managers produce OASs is not to say that each one will produce the same OAS for the same security.

Different manager models build in different prepayment assumptions and use different inputs. For example, a manager model might take into account interest rates (as they affect refinancing), the age of a pool of mortgages (older mortgages are less likely to be prepaid), seasonality (people tend to move during particular periods, such as the summer months), or the slope of the yield curve (which measures the propensity to refinance over a shorter period than the original mortgage). Some managers believe that they can accurately predict prepayments. Others, thinking that this is nearly impossible, strive to reduce prepayment risk through hedging. In any case, different models produce different OASs.

Most MBS managers rank their universe of mortgage-backed securities by their OASs and then concentrate on the upper echelon. A large number of interest-rate scenarios covering the life of the security are usually examined in order to produce a statistically sound OAS. Most manager models are based on certain assumptions about the effect that a change in interest rates or other key variables would have on the level of prepayments. To avoid depending too heavily on the these assumptions, some managers will "stress-test" their assumptions by adjusting the original prepayment assumptions upward and downward, to see what effect these changes have on a security's OAS. Securities that do not show a lot of deterioration when the assumptions are changed are usually deemed to be the most stable.

Information Systems

Because of the complexity and vast number of possible interest rate and prepayment scenarios that MBS managers must consider, powerful computing systems are a veritable must. Generally, the more computing power the better, but computing power by itself, without an effective model, is worthless. MBS managers derive information on MBSs and other fixed-income securities from MBS dealers, Intex, Bloomberg, Reuters, and other sources, and input it into their models.

RISKS AND RISK CONTROL

MBS managers add value by measuring and managing risk through hedging techniques and prudent use of leverage. MBS managers who do not use hedging as part of their strategies should be considered as a separate class. The most common risk factors that managers examine affect the exposure of their portfolio in terms of duration, convexity, prepayments, and yield curve positioning.

Duration

Duration, in general fixed-income terms, is a measure of the sensitivity of a bond's price to a shift in interest rates. For example, if a bond has a duration of three years, then the bond's value will decline approximately 3 percent for each 1 percent increase in interest rates, or will rise approximately 3 percent for each 1 percent fall in interest rates. Such a bond is less risky than a bond with a six-year duration, which will decline in value approximately 6 percent for each 1 percent increase in interest rates, and will rise approximately 6 percent for each 1 percent decrease. Roughly:

$$\text{Duration} = \frac{\text{Change in price / Price}}{\text{Change in interest rates}}.$$

Duration is equal to the average maturity of bonds for which a particular price–yield relationship holds. Bonds with longer maturities will be more affected by a change in interest rates because that change will be felt over a longer period of time. For example, an investor buys a two-year bond with a coupon rate of 7 percent and a five-year bond of similar credit quality with a similar rate of 7 percent. Subsequently, interest rates rise 1 percent. Both bonds are now less attractive than when they were bought, because the investor could now get the same interest rate for less money. The price of the two-year bond, however, reflects the present value of its now less favorable rate over only two years, whereas the five-year bond reflects the present value of its rate over five years. Accordingly, everything else being equal, the price of the bond with the longer maturity will be more sensitive to changes in interest rates. Of course, MBS securities are also affected by changes in prepayments due to changes in interest rates; thus, most managers use "effective duration," a measure of duration that takes into account prepayment activity.

Effective and Partial Duration

Effective duration is the sensitivity of the price of the security to a change in interest rates, adjusted for changes in prepayments. (One might think of it as an "option-adjusted duration.") Effective duration is the measure of duration that MBS managers try to hedge against. They sell short Treasury securities of similar maturities in order to produce a net duration close to zero. Like fixed-income arbitrageurs, MBS arbitrage managers buy an MBS bond and sell short another bond (usually a Treasury bond) with similar duration. If interest rates change, the effect on the long position will be offset by the short position because both bonds respond the same way to the change. If the total duration of the long side of a portfolio is equal to the total duration of the short side of the portfolio, then the portfolio is said to have zero duration. MBS managers may try to eliminate market risk by structuring their trades and portfolios to be at or near zero duration.

Partial duration, a further measure of duration used by some managers, is calculated across the yield curve. This entails a separate duration calculation for one-year, two-year, five-year, 10-year, and 30-year Treasuries. Managers who use partial duration calculations may hedge them with Treasuries across the yield curve if the duration of the security in relation to the different portions of the Treasury yield curve differs significantly. Partial duration calculations are an essential part of parallel and rotational yield curve shift calculations.

Parallel and Rotational Shifts of the Yield Curve

MBS arbitrage managers often attempt to insulate their portfolios from both parallel and rotational shifts in the Treasury yield curve. Their calculations make use of partial durations to indicate the appropriate mix of Treasuries needed to maintain neutrality. Parallel duration calculations estimate the sensitivity of the price of the portfolio with respect to uniform parallel shifts of the Treasury yield curve of different magnitudes. Rotational duration calculations estimate the sensitivity of the price of the portfolio to yield-curve pivots of various magnitudes. (A pivot is achieved by holding one point on the curve constant while changing another.)

Convexity

Convexity measures the degree to which duration changes as a bond's yield to maturity changes. Many managers use convexity as a measure of prepayment risk and try to hedge against it accordingly.

Prepayment Duration

Prepayment duration isolates price sensitivity to moves in prepayment rates, independent of other variables. Because this calculation is difficult to explicitly hedge, it is often used as a reference point that is monitored.

Leverage

Many MBS relative value trades derive returns from the spread between a long MBS position and a short position in Treasury or Treasury-like securities of similar maturity and duration. Because the spread between the two securities is sometimes quite small, these may be leveraged to produce the desired return. But although leverage can increase returns, excessive amounts can put the manager at risk for margin calls and forced selling.

Pricing

Because all mortgage-backed securities are over-the-counter (OTC) instruments, pricing them can be somewhat subjective. The only price that matters is the one someone will pay. Managers use many different techniques to price their portfolios. An in-house model method of pricing securities is the most dubious because, at the end of the day, the only arbiter of price is the market. Some managers use the repurchase market and dealers to price the securities they hold. (The repurchase market determines what value a dealer would assign to the securities in the portfolio if the manager tried to borrow against his or her holdings.) Similarly, some managers send out bid lists to dealers, and ask for bid prices. Managers using this pricing technique usually take into account at least two dealers' bids.

SOURCE OF RETURN

Mortgage-backed securities arbitrage can be included in a discussion of market-neutral strategies because of its emphasis on deriving returns from *the relationship between an undervalued mortgage security and a corresponding hedge constructed with U.S. Treasuries.* The hedge is usually constructed so the trade has zero duration—or, in other words, is indifferent to the moves in interest rates that affect all fixed-income securities alike. In essence, the manager isolates the spread between the two securities and makes returns when that relationship returns to its projected level. Thus, the source of return is driven by relative valuations rather than market direction. But although relative valuation is the driving force behind MBS arbitrage returns, a number of other factors contribute.

Valuation Models

Given that relative valuation drives MBS arbitrage returns, valuation models are essential to manager success. In addition to the traditional factors that affect fixed-income pricing, mortgage-backed models must incorporate assumptions about the current and future levels of prepayments and what the option to prepay is worth. A well-thought-out valuation model allows an MBS arbitrage manager to take advantage of what some managers refer to as the "complexity premium." When they use this phrase, they are implying that the difficulty in valuing MBS securities ensures that there will always be relative misvaluations within the sector.

Leverage

Leverage can increase returns, but it can also put a manager at risk for margin calls that might force the manager to sell securities at disadvantageous prices. Such was the case for Ellington Partners, one of the largest MBS hedge funds, in October 1998. Ellington was highly leveraged when it received margin calls and was forced to sell a large portion of its multibillion-dollar portfolio in order to meet them. Other managers who feared a similar fate and wanted to remain as liquid as possible were reluctant to buy Ellington's securities. The result was a market flooded with securities and devoid of buyers. This excess supply without corresponding demand forced prices of MBS securities down significantly. Because it was forced to sell during this period, Ellington lost over 30 percent during October alone.

Liquidity

Under normal market circumstances, liquidity in the MBS market depends on what type of securities the manager invests in. At a general level, agency securities are almost always more liquid than nonagency securities. Agency securities, to a certain extent, provide better collateral protection. In addition, securities based on pools of single-family-residence mortgages are generally more liquid than those based on pools of commercial mortgages. Home mortgage pools are considered less volatile and less prone to prepayments than commercial mortgages. At a security-specific level, pass-through securities are the most liquid. They are followed by some of the more straightforward CMOs, such as PAC bonds. Liquidity can be a problem with some of the more esoteric CMOs. Managers holding these securities will earn a liquidity risk premium, but, if the liquidity dries up, they may get stuck with a security that they cannot sell at any cost.

Financing

Because most MBS arbitrage strategies take the form of spread trades where the spread is not particularly large, the trades must be leveraged, often significantly, to produce a competitive return. Therefore, MBS arbitrage managers must be able to obtain attractive financing. To establish the credit lines and counterparty relationships that MBS arbitrage strategies require, a manager must have a relatively large minimum amount of capital under management (generally, $25 to $50 million).

Hedging Techniques

Hedging activities can be a drag on returns when the market is moving in the manager's favor, but they are essential to provide downside protection and insulate an MBS manager's portfolio from systemic changes in interest rates. Hedging techniques differ. Some managers hedge using 10-year Treasuries; others use 30-year Treasuries or hedge across the Treasury curve. In addition, some managers use swaps, options, and futures contracts to construct their hedges. It can be difficult to construct hedges for some of the more illiquid MBS instruments.

RECENT DEVELOPMENTS IN MBS ARBITRAGE

After exhibiting stellar risk-adjusted performance throughout the 1990s, many MBS arbitrageurs found the third and fourth quarters of 1998 to be disastrous. The managers included in the HFRI Fixed Income Mortgage-Backed Index averaged –1.17 percent returns in August, –2.15 percent in September, –9.24 percent in October, and –9.18 percent for the year. These numbers, which include only a subset of hedge fund managers who employed the strategy, may mask even more damage done to cross-arbitrage players and other participants in the market. One manager described the circumstances as "the 10,000-year flood." During this period, the strategy fared as badly as or perhaps worse than any of the other market-neutral strategies. What is important is *why* this occurred.

As background to happenings in the third and fourth quarters of 1998, the MBS market was shaken by a spike in prepayments in the spring of that year. Managers holding securities that did not trade in this period, and utilizing in-house pricing models, may not have marked down their positions enough to reflect the change. Thus, they were hit doubly hard by the extreme conditions in the second half of the year. Mortgage-backed spreads suffered from the overriding flight-to-quality situation that occurred after Russia defaulted on $40 billion of internal debt in mid-August. Spreads on even the most liquid MBS securities blew out to record levels, and illiquid MBS securities became virtually untradable. The situation took on critical proportions with the announcement of the Long-Term Capital Management bailout and the increased uncertainty, in the managerial ranks, about margin calls from lenders. At the same time, mortgage rates fell to 30-year lows, creating further incentive for homeowners to prepay mortgages.

The situation peaked in early October when Ellington Capital, a billion-dollar MBS hedge fund, received margin calls and was forced to liquidate much of its portfolio. Dealers were reluctant buyers, given the backdrop of global financial crisis and a desire to protect their profits and bonuses. Managers who were forced to sell or to de-leverage their portfolios during this period were greeted by a highly illiquid market. After the first round of selling, dealers became even more reluctant to buy securities because they were met with a sellers-only market. Subsequently, dealers reduced prices enormously, and bid–offer spreads widened to almost absurd levels. Managers who were forced to sell securities to meet redemptions or margin calls took heavy realized losses. Furthermore, some managers lost money on Treasury hedges when the Treasury curve exhibited extreme volatility and went through a series of fundamental shifts that did not necessarily mirror what was happening in the mortgage sector.

After the turmoil of 1998, the mortgage market returned to a more positive environment in 1999. Interest rates exhibited an upward trend, and prepayments were reduced significantly. Approaching year-end, interest rates were at their highest levels since 1997 and were set to push higher in 2000. Accordingly, the MBS arbitrage managers included in the HFRI Fixed Income Mortgage-Backed Index produced returns in line with, or higher than, their historical average. The historical returns for the strategy are illustrated in Table 6.2 and Figure 6.1.

Table 6.2   Returns from Investments in Mortgage-Backed Securities, 1993–1999

Number of Funds	Average Size (Millions of $US)	Year	Jan	Feb	Mar	Apr	May
5	52	1993	0.88	1.33	0.76	0.72	0.97
11	39	1994	1.18	1.18	1.00	0.32	0.74
12	32	1995	0.84	1.35	1.40	1.08	0.79
16	65	1996	1.36	1.03	1.37	1.13	1.35
22	160	1997	1.07	1.56	1.22	1.58	1.69
27	188	1998	0.81	1.02	0.69	−0.42	0.19
16	220	1999	1.63	1.23	1.68	1.86	0.22

* Annual represents geometric compounded average.

Figure 6.1   Mortgage-Backed Securities Arbitrage: Growth of $1,000, January 1993–December 1999

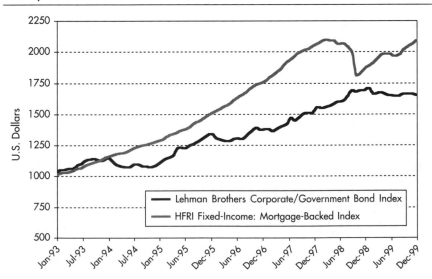

Jun	Jul	Aug	Sep	Oct	Nov	Dec	Annual*
1.45	0.68	1.98	1.41	0.98	0.69	1.82	14.54
1.16	1.47	1.10	0.59	0.69	0.89	0.72	11.61
1.27	1.10	1.14	2.00	1.20	1.42	1.85	16.55
1.51	1.45	1.33	1.58	1.91	1.37	0.49	17.06
2.29	1.37	1.34	1.33	0.98	0.62	1.03	17.31
-1.36	0.17	-1.17	-2.15	-9.24	0.59	1.76	-9.18
-0.12	-0.69	0.49	2.09	1.11	0.91	1.45	12.48

Merger Arbitrage   7

Merger arbitrage usually involves buying the common stock of a company that is being acquired, or merging with another company and selling short the stock of the acquiring company. Some managers may use options rather than stocks if the trade can be done more cheaply that way.

The target company's stock will typically trade at a discount to the value that it will attain after the merger is completed. This occurs because (1) corporate acquisitions are generally made at a premium to the stock price of the target company prior to the announcement of the proposed merger; and (2) all mergers involve event risk—the risk that the transaction will fail to be completed as announced. If the transaction fails to go through, the price of the target company's stock usually declines, sometimes dramatically. Merger arbitrage specialists make profits when they correctly anticipate the outcome of an announced merger and lock in the spread between the current market price of the target company's stock and the amount offered by the acquiring firm.

An impending merger creates a disparity between the price of the acquiring company's stock and the price of the target company's stock. This disparity is referred to as the merger arbitrage spread. As noted above, corporate acquisitions are generally made at a premium to the stock price of the target company, prior to the announcement of the proposed merger. Later in this chapter, some of the factors that affect how large a premium an acquiring firm is willing to pay will be discussed. Common sense tells us, however, that most companies would not accept less than their present market value, as represented by their stock price. Thus, acquiring companies must pay a premium in excess of that stock price.

If the announced deal goes through, stock in the target company will become an ownership interest in the acquiring company. In theory, the two stocks can then be seen to represent ownership interests in the same company. Until the deal is consummated, however, the prices of the two stocks will usually reflect the market's uncertainty about whether the deal will go through. Uncertainty can be generated by any number of factors, including, but not confined to, financing difficulties, regulatory roadblocks, complicated deal structures, management disagreement, market sentiment, and the emergence of new negative information about one of the two firms. Often, the effect is that the target company's stock trades at a discount to the value it will attain if the deal is completed.

Merger arbitrage specialists usually translate an arbitrage spread into an annualized rate of return, estimate the probability that the deal will go through, and then determine whether the returns to be derived from the spread (if the deal is completed) offer sufficient compensation for the estimated risk of the deal's failing. As a general rule, friendly deals involving large-capitalization companies will produce tighter spreads and moderate rates of return. More complex deals, and those involving small-capitalization firms, will usually produce wider spreads and higher rates of return because of their increased risk.

Merger arbitrage specialists do not try to anticipate possible merger activity, because trying to anticipate mergers is to invest on the basis of rumors. Instead, they research announced mergers and acquisitions in order to reduce their uncertainty about each of the possible outcomes. Before taking a position, they will consider public corporate documents of the firms, historical financial statements for each of the firms, EDGAR Fed filings, analysts' reports, standard media releases, conference calls, and conversations with the companies' management and industry contacts. If arbitrageurs feel that the rate of return implicit in the spread is significantly more than the actual risk that the deal will not be completed, they will put on a position. Generally, they will enlarge the position as more nonnegative information becomes available or as market sentiment toward the deal solidifies, making the outcome of the transaction more certain. A merger arbitrage manager will liquidate an investment position when new negative information is uncovered or when the return no longer offers a sufficient reward for the perceived risks of holding the position. But if all goes as planned, the position will not be liquidated until the merger is consummated.

MERGER ARBITRAGE APPROACHES

Cash Mergers or Tender Offers

The simplest example of a merger arbitrage opportunity is a company being acquired for cash. The target company's stock will typically trade slightly below the price proposed by the acquiring company. An investor who purchases the target company's stock will receive this discount when the deal is completed. In effect, the investor receives an "insurance premium" for accepting the risk that the transaction could fail to occur. The source of return in cash merger situations is derived solely from the premium the acquiring firm decides to pay, because the dollar amount of the cash payment will not change between the time the deal is announced and the time the deal is completed. Merger arbitrage specialists will buy the stock of the target company, or an option on that stock, to lock in this differential.

Thus, the manager must research the balance sheets of the two companies in detail, to ensure that the acquiring firm will be able to support the combined entity. The risk to the investor is solely event risk and is unrelated to the prices of the two stocks. Possible stumbling blocks include legal and regulatory issues, market sentiment, and questions about whether the acquiring firm has sufficient cash flow to finance the acquisition.

Stock Swap Mergers

In stock swap mergers, or stock-for-stock mergers, the holders of the target company's stock receive shares of the acquiring company's stock. The majority of mergers during the past few years have been stock-for-stock deals. A merger arbitrage specialist will sell the acquiring company's stock short, and will purchase a long position in the target company, using the same ratio as that of the proposed transaction. (If the purchasing firm is offering a half-share of its stock for every share of the target company, then the merger arbitrageur will sell half as many shares of the purchasing firm as he or she buys of the target company.) By going long and short in this ratio, the manager ensures that the number of shares for which the long position will be swapped is equal to the number of shares sold short. When the deal is completed, the manager will cover the short and collect the spread that has been locked in.

As with all mergers, stock swap mergers involve event risk. Any number of factors can cause a deal to fail to be completed. In addition to the normal event risks, stock swap mergers involve risks associated with fluctuations in the stock prices of the two companies. Because the terms of the deal involve an exchange of shares and are predicated on the prices of the two companies' stock at the time of the announcement, drastic changes in the share prices of one or both of the companies can cause the entire deal to be reevaluated. Merger arbitrageurs derive returns from stock swap mergers when the spread or potential return justifies the perceived risk of the deal's failing.

Example: Albertson's–American Stores

A good example of a successful stock swap merger is the Albertson's (ABS) and American Stores (ASC) deal that was announced on August 3, 1998, and closed on June 24, 1999. It also illustrates some of the possible event risks that merger arbitrage managers must assess.

At the time of the announcement, ABS was to buy ASC for $11.7 billion in stock and debt, in a move that was intended to create the nation's largest food and drug company. Under the agreement, ASC shareholders were to receive 0.63 share of ABS stock for each share of American they owned. The deal valued American Stores at $30.24 a share, a $7.05 share premium above the stock's $23.19 close on the previous trading day. Albertson's CEO, Gary

Michael, expected that the acquisition would close in the first quarter of 1999 and would add to earnings by the end of 1999. He was quoted as saying that the deal would bring "substantial accretion two to three years out." Combined, the two companies would operate 2,470 stores in 37 states. Annual sales were estimated at $36 billion for 1998. The deal was intended to give Albertson's much more heft in purchasing, a key tool in the low-margin retailing business.

To assess the premium paid, the synergies between the two companies, and the risk that the deal could fall through, the merger arbitrage manager examined both companies' publicly available documents, the terms of the merger, and other happenings in the industry, and consulted with an antitrust lawyer to better understand any legal restrictions on the proposed merger. Although some possibility of antitrust problems was found, the fundamental synergies and the reward offered in the form of the premium outweighed that low-probability risk. The manager locked in the spread by going long ASC and short ABS in the same ratio that was detailed in the merger agreement. The day of the merger announcement, the merger arbitrage manager took the following positions:

August 3, 1998:

Long 10,000 shares of ASC at $24 = $240,000

Short 6,300 shares of ABS at $48 = $302,400

Hedge ratio: 0.63

Subsequent to the announcement of the ASC and ABS merger, two significant events occurred that the manager had to monitor to ensure that his position was as good as initially anticipated. Two other large grocery stores, Kroger and Freddy Meyer, announced that they also would merge. The combined company would be larger than the combined Albertson's and American Stores company. When this deal closed, ABS was under pressure to complete its deal with ASC, in order to compete with the newly combined Kroger

Company. In addition, the ACS and ABS merger became subject to antitrust action because of market crossovers between the two companies, particularly in California. The merger eventually became bogged down in court proceedings, but, because of competitive pressure from the Kroger–Freddy Meyer deal, ASC and ABS made certain compromises in order to complete the deal.

To settle antitrust concerns about overlapping markets resulting from the $12 billion deal, the two companies agreed to sell stores. Under the proposed order, they were forced to sell 144 supermarkets and five planned sites—the largest retail divestiture in the Federal Trade Commission's history. Antitrust regulators had contended that the deal would substantially reduce competition in California, Nevada, and New Mexico. Attorneys general from the three states helped orchestrate the agreement and filed consent decrees in their own federal courts.

The merger closed on June 23, 1999, with ABS at $52. Thus, the 10,000-share long position in ACS, purchased at $24 a share, became a 6,300-share long position in ABS at $52, for a profit of $87,600.

The 6,300 shares of ABS sold short at $48 were covered at $52 for a loss of $25,200.

Total profit on the trade was $62,400, and the rate of return was roughly 26 percent ($62,400/$240,000).

Stock Swap Mergers with a Collar

Stock swap mergers are often even more complex when the exchange ratio is based on the price of the acquiring company's stock when the deal is closed, or, in a more extreme case, when the target firm can call off the merger if the acquiring firm's stock price falls below a certain floor, or "collar." Because the merger's completion is explicitly linked to the stock price of the acquiring firm, stock swap mergers with collars are more sensitive to stock market volatility than other merger arbitrage opportunities.

In deals that can be called off if the acquiring firm's price falls below the collar, market risk is explicitly translated into event risk. A spate of stock market volatility can cause merger arbitrageurs involved in such deals either to adjust their hedges to reflect new exchange ratios, or to unwind positions that are no longer attractive or have fallen through on the basis of a movement in the stock price of the acquiring company. On the other hand, because a collar can be structured to ensure that the target company receives a fair price, the collar may actually decrease the risk of the deal's falling through. The outcome of more complex mergers is generally more uncertain; therefore, their spreads will usually be larger.

Merger arbitrage managers usually look at collar deals in one of two ways:

1. They assign probabilities to each possible scenario and then calculate a rate of return based on the exchange ratios and the probabilities. For example, if a collar stipulates three possible scenarios, with a different exchange ratio for each, the manager could look at the rate of return that would occur in each of the three scenarios, multiply those rates of return by the probability of that scenario's occurring, and come up with a rate of return calculation for the deal as a whole.

2. They analyze a collar as an option. If the acquiring company trades down through the bottom of the collar, the manager loses the optionality and the position becomes directional; that is, the manager holds an unhedged long position in the target company.

Example: WorldCom–SkyTel

An example of a stock swap merger with a collar is the merger of SkyTel (SKYT) and MCI Worldcom (WCOM), announced

May 28, 1999. SkyTel is a wireless messaging company that serves over 1.6 million customers. Since 1989, the company has participated in an industry-wide push toward nationwide messaging. SkyTel has been responsible for a number of wireless messaging innovations, culminating in a two-way interactive messaging service that enables customers to exchange messages with the Internet and other pagers, receive messages via e-mail and the Internet, and send messages to any telephone in the United States. SkyTel had $518 million in revenue in 1998.

MCI WorldCom is a global communications services company with operations in more than 65 countries encompassing the Americas, Europe, and the Asia–Pacific regions. The company provides facilities-based and fully integrated local, long-distance, international, and Internet services. MCI WorldCom's networks, which include a pan-European network and a transoceanic cable system, provide high-capacity connectivity to more than 40,000 buildings throughout the world. The company is currently making a push to provide broadband access through traditional copper phone lines via digital subscriber line (DSL) technology, to supplement its existing fiber-optic network. A second medium for broadband delivery will be satellite dishes on homes (referred to in the industry as MMDS) that can provide service to rural areas beyond traditional phone lines. In 1998, MCI WorldCom had revenues of more than $30 billion. MCI WorldCom and SkyTel are both headquartered in Mississippi, and MCI WorldCom is currently the largest reseller of SkyTel services.

Three days prior to the announcement of the merger, Company Sleuth, a free online business service of Infonautics (INFO), discovered that MCI Worldcom had registered the Internet domain *skytel worldcom.com*. SkyTel's stock rose as much as 16 percent, based on the news of the Web site address registration. MCI WorldCom spokesperson Barbara Gibson declined to comment on whether the companies were in merger talks. "But I can tell you that its registration had absolutely nothing to do with whether the two companies are in merger talks or not," she said in an interview on May 25, 1999. Scott Hamilton, vice president of investor relations for SkyTel, also declined to comment on any merger talks. At the close of that trading day, SkyTel shares were up 1¼ to 20⅛ and WorldCom shares were up ⅛ to 83¼.

On May 28, WorldCom and SkyTel announced a definitive agreement to merge the two companies. MCI WorldCom told analysts that the deal would help the telecom giant explore new opportunities in wireless services, reinforcing the company's push to diversify beyond its core long-distance and Internet businesses. CEO Bernard Ebbers said of the deal: "It's a foundation to deploy other wireless services." The company further stated that it believed the deal would enhance earnings immediately after closing. In an interview on June 2, 1999, Vice Chairman John Skidmore said he envisions consumers of the future carrying up to as many as five wireless appliances at a time, ranging from Palm Pilots to pagers, cellular phones, and newer products not yet available to consumers.

The terms of the deal were as follows:

- Holders of SkyTel common stock were entitled to receive shares of MCI WorldCom common stock for each share of SkyTel common stock. Based on the average trading price for MCI WorldCom common stock on May 27, the merger valued each share of SkyTel common stock at $21.24.

- The common stock exchange ratio would be fixed at 0.25 share of MCI WorldCom common stock for each share of SkyTel common stock, so long as the average trading price for MCI WorldCom common stock was greater than $80.00 per share during the 20 trading days ending three trading days prior to the closing of the merger.

- If MCI WorldCom's average trading price was between $72.00 and $80.00 per share, the exchange ratio would be increased to a number of MCI WorldCom shares equal to $20.00 divided by the average price.

- If the average trading price for MCI WorldCom common shares was less than $72.00 per share, the exchange ratio would be fixed at 0.2778 share of MCI WorldCom common stock for each share of SkyTel common stock.

- Based on WorldCom's share price at the time of the announcement ($84.96), the offering of $21.24 per share of SkyTel stock represented a 5 percent premium to SkyTel's stock price at the time of the announcement ($20.23).

These terms created four possible scenarios:

Scenario 1. WorldCom's stock trades above the collar, and each SkyTel share is exchanged for 0.25 share of WorldCom stock. This scenario seemed very probable because of the underlying fundamental strength of WorldCom's business and the synergies between the two firms. Investors would have been unlikely to drive WorldCom's price down because they didn't like the merger. It would most likely have taken bad fundamental news to cause the price of WorldCom's stock to fall below 80. The manager assigned this scenario a probability of 0.60.

Scenario 2. WorldCom's stock trades within the collar, and each SkyTel share is exchanged for a number of WorldCom shares equal to 20 divided by the WorldCom stock price (the range of ratios is 0.25 to 0.277). This scenario was less likely than Scenario 1, given the strength of WorldCom's underlying business and its excellent reputation with Wall Street analysts. Adverse happenings in the industry in general, such as a bad earnings report by another big name like AT&T, could conceivably have caused the whole sector to trade down and make this scenario more likely. The manager assigned this scenario a probability of 0.27.

Scenario 3. WorldCom's stock trades below 72 and each SkyTel share is exchanged for 0.278 share of WorldCom. This scenario would have required either disappointing fundamental news from WorldCom or a systematic decline of stock prices in the telecommunications sector. The manager assigned this scenario a probability of 0.08.

Scenario 4. The deal does not get completed. At the time of the announcement, the only obstacles to the deal's getting done were FCC approval and the approval of shareholders. The deal did not seem to present any possible antitrust difficulties. It appeared that only very bad fundamental news from one of the companies could stop it from completion. The manager assigned this scenario a probability of 0.05.

The manager locked in the highly probable Scenario 1 spread by going long SKYT and short WCOM in a ratio of 4 to 1. On May 28, the manager took the following positions:

Long: 20,000 shares of SKYT@ $20.50

Short: 5,000 shares of WCOM@ $85.00

Exchange ratio: 0.25

The manager monitored the stock prices of the two companies. If WCOM traded into the collar, he was ready to adjust his hedge ratio to reflect the new exchange ratio. In addition, he closely monitored news items regarding the status of the merger, the fundamentals of the two companies, and any changes that might affect the outcome of the deal.

The merger closed on October 1, 1999, with WCOM at $72. The average trading price of WCOM during the previous 20-day period was equal to $78, setting the exchange ratio at 0.2566. Thus, the 20,000-share long position in Skytel purchased at

$20.50 a share became a 5,132-share long position in WCOM at $72 for a loss of $40,496.

The 5,000 shares of WCOM sold short at $85 were covered at $72, for a profit of $65,000.

Total profit on the trade was $24,504, and the rate of return for the four-month period was roughly 5.98 percent ($24,504/$410,000).

Multiple Bidder Situations

A more complex deal involved Global Crossing (GBLX), which announced merger agreements first with Frontier (FRO) and then with U.S. West (USW). The Global–Frontier deal included a collar and the option for Frontier to buy out of the deal if Global traded through the lower end of the collar. The U.S. West deal called for a cash tender offer by U.S. West for 39 million shares of Global stock. Subsequent to the tender offer and final approval, the two companies would merge.

Further complicating the deal, the combined company, which would retain the name Global Crossing, would create two classes of stock. The G (global) class would track the high-growth global fiber-optic and bandwidth provider businesses of Global Crossing and Frontier. The L (local) class would track the more established traditional local and long-distance telephone businesses of U.S. West and Frontier. As if this wasn't complicated enough, shortly after the announcement of these deals, a Global competitor, Qwest (QWST), announced rival unsolicited bids for both Frontier and U.S. West at a premium to Global's offers. The large premium immediately shrank when Qwest shares lost 20 percent on the heels of the announcement. Qwest proceeded to sweeten its deal by offering Frontier and U.S. West provisions that would protect them from stock price volatility. In the end, Global Crossing retained its agreement with Frontier, and Qwest lured away U.S. West.

Global Crossing–Frontier Deal

The complicated deal began on March 17, 1999, when Global Crossing announced that it would buy Frontier Corporation, a phone company based in Rochester, New York, in a deal valued at about $11.2 million. Global Crossing, a telecommunications company, was putting together the world's first independent global fiber-optic network. Frontier was the sixth largest long-distance company in the United States.

The number of Global Crossing shares to be received by Frontier shareholders was to be adjusted to produce a value of $62 per Frontier share, as long as Global Crossing shares traded within a range of $34.56 to $56.78 per share (the collar) during a pricing period prior to closing. Outside the collar, Frontier shareholders would receive a fixed number of Global Crossing shares: 1.0919 shares at the top end of the collar and 1.7939 shares at the bottom of the collar. If Global Crossing shares traded below the bottom collar, Frontier could walk away from the deal if it gave $275 million to Global Crossing.

On the news of Global Crossing's agreement to buy Frontier, Global's stock price fell into the mid-30s. Investors started to worry that the deal did not make sense. More important, word spread that one or both companies had accounting problems. Both companies categorically denied the charge. Global's stock price subsequently rebounded to levels higher than when the deal was announced.

From a merger arbitrage standpoint, the deal involved a number of risks. A large number of state agencies had to sign off on it. In the meantime, Global Crossing had to exhibit sound fundamental business strategies and try not to unleash any earnings surprises. In 1998, Global Crossing lost about $88 million. In 1999, it was expected to net $0.03 per share.

Arbitrageurs would consider taking these risks if they were able to construct a typical hedge—buy the target and short the acquirer.

However, they found it very hard to borrow Global Crossing shares, which made it nearly impossible to short them.

Global Crossing–U.S. West Deal

On May 17, U.S. West Inc., a Baby Bell phone company, reached an agreement to merge with Global Crossing. The deal called for U.S. West to purchase 9.5 percent of Global Crossing for roughly $2.4 billion. The two companies would then merge in a 50–50 stock combination, creating a company with $17 billion in annual revenue and a stock market value of $65 billion. The deal was valued at $37 million at the time of the announcement.

The combined company, which would keep the Global Crossing name, would have two separate stocks: one to track the performance of the high-growth Internet and data assets (G class), and one for the traditional telephone assets (L class). Investors were to choose which stock they wanted to hold.

Robert Annunziata, Global Crossing's CEO, was to share the power and the top title of the new company with Solomon Trujillo, the chief executive of U.S. West. The board of directors was to include ten members from each company, plus two chosen by mutual agreement. "A decade and a half after the breakup of AT&T, competition in the telecommunications industry has spread around the world," Annunziata said in a statement. "Today we are joining forces with a former regional Bell operating company that knows how to compete."

U.S. West, based in Denver, had local phone customers in fourteen western and midwestern states, plus a wireless phone service, and it offered high-speed Internet access. It had $12.4 billion in revenue in 1998.

The U.S. West deal was less well received by investors than the Frontier deal. Analysts voiced concern that the traditional telephone emphasis of U.S. West would dilute the high-growth

Internet and data businesses that formed the core of Global Cross-ing. Global's stock traded back down into the 40s on the news of the deal. At the time, investors voiced concern that if Global's stock continued to trade down because of the U.S. West deal, the Frontier deal might be jeopardized.

From a merger arbitrage perspective, the Global–U.S. West deal contained a number of unique risks because of the complexity of the arrangement. First, the deal was dependent on the success-ful completion of the Frontier deal. Second, the creation of two tracking stocks presented some problems. Investors might respond negatively to the idea of the two stocks, and, regardless, would probably demand more of the G shares than the L shares.

Qwest–U.S. West–Frontier Deal

To complicate matters further, on June 14, a Global rival, Qwest (QWST), made unsolicited takeover offers for Frontier and U.S. West. Qwest and Global Crossing were both erecting worldwide fiber-optic cable networks to capitalize on the soaring demand for high-speed data, Internet, e-mail, and other telecommunications services. Yet both companies were only three years old and lacked the large numbers of customers and recognizable brands needed to challenge the likes of AT&T and MCI WorldCom.

Qwest offered 1.738 shares of its stock for each share of U.S. West stock. For Frontier, Qwest offered $20 plus 1.181 Qwest shares for each Frontier share. The combined deal was worth some $55 billion at the time of the announcement. Subsequent to the announcement, investors drove the price of Qwest's stock down 25 percent, reducing the total value of the deal to $41.5 billion and wiping out the premium above Global Crossing's offer. In the days that followed, both U.S. West and Frontier stated that they were sticking to their agreements with Global Crossing. The companies were concerned about the volatility of Qwest's stock price and the continuation of current expansion strategies under the combined company.

Undeterred by rebuffs from both the market and the takeover targets, Qwest CEO Joseph Nacchio sent letters to each company, urging discussions. On June 23, Qwest revised its original terms. Qwest now offered to pay $69 a share for stock in U.S. West, and $68 a share in cash and stock for Frontier. The deal included a collar that locked those prices in place as long as Qwest shares traded between $43.50 and $30.40. The new offer represented a 12 percent premium to Global Crossing's offer. Both U.S. West and Frontier entered into discussions with Qwest.

From a merger arbitrage standpoint, multiple bidder situations are a double edged sword. Although they create higher premiums, they make it difficult to construct a hedge because of uncertainty about which buyer will win the bidding war. In addition, targets may have to buy out of their existing merger agreements, so a larger premium must be more than the amount of the buyout, in order to make sense. In this case, U.S. West was required to pay Global about $750 million when it broke the deal. On December 31, U.S. West sold 65 percent of its stake in Global Crossing, to take advantage of a rise in Global Crossing's share price. The sale involved about 24 million shares, valued at $1.15 billion (an average of $47.92 per share). The sale marked a step toward disentangling Global Crossing from U.S. West. At this writing, the Qwest–U.S. West deal has been approved by shareholders, and seems to be moving toward a mid-2000 close.

Outcome of Global Crossing–Frontier Deal

Frontier retained its merger agreement with Global Crossing. The agreement was reworked to reflect the decline in Global's stock price: Each share of Frontier was exchanged for 2.05 shares of Global Crossing. After this announcement, shares of Global became easier to short, and the deal traded in a less complicated fashion. The merger closed on September 28, 1999. Global Crossing's shares rallied as much as 150 percent from their September low of $20.25.

Leveraged Buyouts and Hostile Takeovers

Leveraged buyouts (LBOs) are a type of merger that was created in the 1980s. Michael Milken became the most prominent financial persona of the decade by financing corporate raids with the issuance of junk (high yield, low credit quality) bonds. Notable corporate raiders such as Ron Perelman, Boone Pickens, Nelson Peltz, and Sir James Goldsmith sold junk bonds through Milken's Drexel Burnham Lambert to raise the money to take over companies such as Revlon, TWA, Disney, and Union Carbide. As Edward Chancellor has noted, "The purpose of the leveraged buyout . . . was to acquire a company with the maximum amount of debt. The interest and principal on the LBO debt was to be paid off as quickly as possible with the cash flow generated by the company."[1] Debt was said to force the new owners of the company to "trim the fat" off the company, which often meant replacing existing management.

Conventional valuations gave way to calculations of how much cash flow a company could generate and how much debt it could service. If the company could generate enough cash flow to service the debt, then the raider had effectively bought a company with borrowed money, and would finance the borrowing with the cash flow generated by that same company. In the 1980s, notable so-called "arbitrageurs" such as Ivan Boesky tried to identify companies that were vulnerable to a leveraged takeover and then took a stake in those companies, hoping to receive the premium paid by

---

[1] Edward Chancellor, *Devil Take the Hindmost: A History of Financial Speculation* (New York: 1999), p. 255.

the corporate raider. In retrospect, arbitrage was a misnomer for these individuals' behavior, which was highly speculative.

The era of leveraged buyouts and corporate raiders came to a halt in the early 1990s—beginning with the failure of a number of prominent thrifts, and culminating in Milken's being sentenced to jail for 10 years. The loopholes that allowed Milken to issue large amounts of junk bonds to finance raids have been closed. But, although LBOs have become less common, the form still persists. Disciplined merger arbitrageurs will only consider announced deals, and they refrain from the speculative behavior exhibited by Boesky and other so-called arbitrageurs in the 1980s.

In an LBO, the acquiring company will still use leverage (borrowed funds) to produce the cash necessary to buy the target firm. To attract the funds necessary to finance the acquisition, the acquiring company may issue junk bonds. Because LBOs are not generally friendly transactions, the target company will often fight the deal and demand larger premiums. These deals involve risks that are entirely different from those in cash or stock mergers. They include the financial strain on the acquiring firm when it must borrow funds at high interest rates, and the unwillingness of the target company's management to accept the takeover bid.

Because LBOs are often financed by issuing debt, a merger arbitrageur must do a fundamental credit analysis of the firm to determine whether servicing that debt endangers the completion of the acquisition. LBOs and hostile takeover situations create larger spreads. They promise greater returns than standard mergers, but they also create a flood of risks that the merger arbitrageur may or may not be willing to analyze.

Example: Allied Waste–Browning-Ferris Industries

Allied Waste provides collection, recycling, and disposal services for residential, commercial, industrial, and medical waste customers.

Browning-Ferris Industries also provides collection, recycling, and disposal services for residential, commercial, industrial, and medical waste customers. On March 8, 1999, Allied Waste (AW) announced that it would acquire Browning-Ferris Industries (BFI) for $9.4 billion in cash and assumption of debt, in a deal that combined the nation's second and third largest trash-hauling companies. Allied Waste was the smaller of the two companies, but it financed the acquisition by issuing some $1.6 billion worth of convertible preferred stock and obtaining $9.5 billion in senior financing from a bank group led by the Chase Manhattan Bank. The deal called for Allied to assume $1.8 billion in debt and to pay $45 a share for Browning-Ferris—a 29 percent premium to BFI's stock price at the time of the announcement. Allied Waste expected the acquisition to add to earnings by the year 2000.

In addition to the more standard analysis of synergies between the two companies and possible antitrust obstacles, the deal involved different risks than a "plain vanilla" stock swap or cash merger. Among them were the financial strain on the acquiring firm, created by borrowing funds at high interest rates, and the willingness of BFI's management to accept the takeover bid, perhaps because of the 29 percent per-share premium that Allied offered. Because the deal was financed primarily through debt issuance, a merger arbitrageur would have done a fundamental credit analysis of the firm to determine whether servicing that debt would endanger the completion of the acquisition. The AW–BFI deal is a good example of how LBO situations create larger spreads that promise greater returns, but also carry unusual risks that the merger arbitrageur may or may not want to accept.

A merger arbitrageur who deemed the event risk small enough to justify the position went long BFI, locking in the premium received when the deal was completed.

On March 8, the manager put on the following position:

Long: 20,000 shares of BFI at $36

When the deal closed, the manager was assured to receive $45 for each share, or a 25 percent return. The merger arbitrageur monitored fundamental news for both companies, antitrust developments regarding the proposed deal, and other events that could affect the deal.

On April 9, Allied Waste and Browning Ferris Industries completed an asset swap to settle a lawsuit brought by the Department of Justice, and eliminated the deal's potential harm to competition.

On April 15, Allied Waste announced the signing of a definitive agreement with Stericycle under which Stericycle would purchase all of the medical waste assets that Allied was to acquire through its acquisition of BFI. "The proposed sale of BFI's medical waste operations is consistent with Allied's intent to divest assets and operations which are not strategic to its core solid waste business and to utilize the proceeds to reduce the company's debt as a result of the BFI acquisition," said Ton Van Weelden, Chairman, President, and CEO of Allied Waste.[2]

In late April, both Allied and BFI reported first-quarter earnings in line with analysts' expectations.

On July 7, the largest company in the waste management sector, Waste Management Inc. (WMI), warned that its second-quarter earnings would be some 7 cents a share below analysts' estimates. WMI's stock price plummeted 36 percent on the news. BFI and AW stocks dipped slightly in sympathy, but it would seem that BFI and/or AW had likely picked up some of WMI's lost market share.

On August 2, Allied Waste announced that the deal had been closed. Owners of Browning-Ferris shares received $45 a share in cash. Having bought at $36, the merger arbitrageur made $9 a share, or 25 percent above what he had paid for the shares.

---

[2] PR Newswire, April 15, 1999.

RISKS

Event Risk

The primary risk to all merger arbitrage strategies is event risk. When an announced deal falls through, the merger arbitrageur's long position in the target company will generally drop significantly, erasing the expected premium. The merger between Ciena and Tellabs, announced on June 3, 1998, and annulled on September 14, 1998, is a good example of a high-profile deal that fell through, even though a lot of merger arbitrage strategists liked it.

The Ciena–Tellabs Failed Deal

Ciena, of Linthicum, Maryland, makes equipment that lets fiber-optic lines carry up to 40 times more voice and data traffic, without a need to install more lines. The technology, known as Dense Wavelength Division Multiplexing (DWDM), allows telecommunications carriers to get more bandwidth out of one fiber-optic route, without installing extra cables. The company had about $373 million in revenues in 1997.

Tellabs, based in Lisle, Illinois, makes digital "cross-connect" systems that link incoming and outgoing lines, and systems that allow many signals to travel over a single circuit. Tellabs had about $1.2 billion in revenue in 1997. On June 3, 1998, Tellabs announced that it would buy Ciena in a stock-for-stock deal valued at $7.1 billion, based on Tellabs's stock price of 65¾ at the time of the announcement. Under the original merger agreement, each share of Ciena would have been exchanged for a share of Tellabs. This represented about a 14 percent premium over Ciena's share price.

The deal was intended to position the combined company to take on larger rival equipment makers such as Lucent Technologies.

Tellabs would gain an edge with Ciena's customer base, which included two telecommunications providers, WorldCom and Sprint. "As competition among service providers continues to heighten, equipment suppliers must help both incumbent and newly established carriers meet the demands for increasing and effectively managing the bandwidth in their networks," said Michael Birck, president and CEO of Tellabs. Ciena president and CEO Patrick Nettles said, "We expect the new combined company to accelerate the pace of evolution and the speed of revolution in the public networks." Tellabs expected the deal to dilute its 1998 earnings slightly. The deal was well received by Wall Street and the merger arbitrage community alike.[3]

A merger arbitrage manager might have taken the following positions on June 3 or soon thereafter:

Long: 10,000 shares of Ciena at $59

Short: 10,000 shares of Tellabs at $63

Hedge ratio: 1:1

Ciena's stock traded as high as 90 during the summer. One week before the shareholder meetings on the deal were to be held, CEOs Birck and Nettles, in a joint conference call, reaffirmed that the deal would close in a week. Then, on August 21, the day the Ciena shareholder meeting was to be held, AT&T announced its decision to drop consideration of Ciena's Dense Wavelength Division Multiplexing systems. Ciena shares fell 45 percent on the news, and the shareholder meeting was postponed. In addition, Ciena issued a warning that third-quarter results would be weaker than expected.

---

[3] CNN, June 3, 1998.

To calm anxious shareholders and rally support for the merger, the deal was reworked by August 28. Each share of Ciena would be converted to 0.8 share of Tellabs. Ciena's shares rebounded, but the deal still needed to be approved by the shareholders. In the meantime, Ciena lost another major contract with one of its customers, Digital Teleport.

On September 14, the deal broke. Ciena's shares were trading at close to $15, and Tellabs shareholders were not willing to pay $37 a share for a company they could buy in the market for $15. Tellabs shares also fell some 16 percent to $38, on a warning of weaker-than-expected earnings.

A merger arbitrage manager closing out the position on September 14 would have incurred the following losses:

Sell: 10,000 shares of Ciena at $15 for a loss of $44,000

Buy: 10,000 shares of Tellabs at $40 for a gain of $23,000

Net loss: $21,000 loss/$59,000 original capital = −35.66 percent

Deal Flow

The quantity of announced deals is cyclical and can be affected by economic conditions. For example, in the fall of 1998, very few deals were announced. Potential buyers waited to pursue mergers or acquisitions until uncertainty about global financial and political stability had waned. Merger arbitrageurs are constrained by the quality and quantity of announced deals.

Liquidity

Liquidity is not usually a problem because all merger arbitrage trades involve equities. However, deals involving small-capitalization companies may be subject to some liquidity risk.

RISK CONTROL

Diversification

One way in which merger arbitrage managers control event risk is through diversification. If they can put together a diversified portfolio of merger arbitrage trades, then the failure of one deal will not spell disaster for the portfolio as a whole. Many managers use position limits to control the size of any one position in their portfolio. The ability to diversify is somewhat dependent on the quality and quantity of announced deal flow.

Leverage

Many merger arbitrage managers use some amount of leverage. When used prudently, leverage increases the risk of these trades only in proportion to the amount of leverage used. But, as witnessed in the third quarter of 1998, when a portfolio of merger arbitrage trades is supported almost entirely by borrowed funds, it can become very risky. Nobody knows exactly how extensive Long Term Capital Management's merger arbitrage portfolio was, but it is clear that it was large and was supported almost entirely by leverage. The firm was eventually forced to unwind its positions (many of them at huge losses), so that it could provide the liquidity needed to support other parts of its portfolio.

SOURCE OF RETURN

In a normal market environment, merger arbitrage returns are event-driven (rather than market-driven) because merger arbitrageurs take long positions in target companies and sell short acquiring companies. The ratio they use locks in the spread between the two companies that will eventually become one company, and they receive the premium paid by the acquiring company for taking the risk that the deal may fall through. Merger arbitrage returns, therefore, are not strongly correlated to overall stock market movement under most stock market conditions, because they are derived from *the relationship between the stock prices of two companies.*

However, this general statement about the source of return must be qualified. Merger arbitrage returns are determined by deal spreads and the amount of deal flow, both of which are related to the directional fortunes of the stock market. Deal flow can slow down or disappear in market corrections. Similarly, acquiring companies are more likely to pay larger premiums during bull markets, when high stock prices provide ready currency for mergers and acquisitions.

The strategy is subject to its own set of risks. Generally, these are event risks having to do with *the relationship between the target company and the buyer,* rather than directional risks having to do with the systematic direction of stock market prices. Nonetheless, merger arbitrage specialists can achieve ample and stable returns, over time, based on their ability to anticipate the probable outcomes of specific transactions, as opposed to the far more random nature of most directional investment strategies.

The research process that merger arbitrageurs use to examine possible investment is the same in any market. Managers examine publicly available documents to assess synergies between acquiring and target companies; estimate the probabilities of possible outcomes of announced deals; analyze possible regulatory roadblocks to a deal's completion; and value the stock of involved companies.

GROWTH AND RECENT DEVELOPMENTS IN MERGER ARBITRAGE

Merger arbitrage as a strategy more than doubled, from less than 1 percent of hedge fund assets in 1990 to over 2 percent in 1999. This growth occurred despite the fact that the strategy is constrained by the number of announced deals and the regulatory environment.

Deal Flow and Other Factors Affecting Volume

Merger arbitrage returns are not highly correlated to overall stock market movements, but they still depend on the overall volume and nature of merger activity at any given time. When deal flow dries up, as it did during the third quarter of 1998 because of worries about global financial and political instability, merger arbitrage managers find it much more difficult to put together a diversified portfolio of trades. As evidenced by the spate of stock-for-stock mergers in the fourth quarter of 1998 and throughout 1999, rising stock prices create opportunities for companies whose stock has been carried upward to use the value of that stock as currency for acquisitions.

Internet stocks are an excellent example of how stock values increase acquisition activity. The demand for Internet stocks has been extraordinary. Investors have been willing to pay previously unheard-of prices to own stock in companies that have yet to register a profit. Big-name companies in the sector, such as America Online and Yahoo!, which have relatively low earnings and relatively high stock prices, have been able to use their stock prices to acquire other large companies such as Netscape and Broadcast.com.

The current bull market has also influenced the nature of announced deal flow. The overall volume of mergers exploded in the 1990s, but, as discussed previously, the number of leveraged buyouts and hostile takeovers funded by junk bonds decreased significantly. The majority of mergers today are strategic and noncompetitive. The acquiring company generally has a sound business reason for the merger.

The number of such transactions has been up in recent years, for two reasons:

1. Bull market stock prices provide readily available currency for stock swap mergers.

2. Companies that are looking to expand increased their efficiency in the early 1990s and have subsequently enjoyed high profitability and strong cash flow. These companies often want to expand into related niches and find that it is cheaper to buy market share than compete for it through the existing business structure.

Companies are also consolidating in response to global competition. Foreign markets are of increasing importance to domestic business health. Regulatory changes can also prompt mergers and acquisitions. A good example is the banking industry, which continues to consolidate as the barriers to interstate commerce collapse. Major deals include First Chicago–Bank One, Deutsche Bank–Bankers Trust, and Bank of America–Nations Bank Montgomery.

Another factor affecting the volume and type of mergers is the changes in management compensation packages. Stock options have become almost expected. Logically, then, managers' interests should be aligned, more closely than ever, with shareholders' interests, because a high percentage of their total compensation is represented by stock options. Executives are more willing to consider business moves (including selling or merging their firms) that will create shareholder value and, in the process, increase their personal wealth. Consider the America Online–Netscape deal announced in November 1998. When the deal was announced, it was a $4 billion deal. By April of 1999, the deal was worth $15 billion because of the rapid increase in the price of America Online's stock in the months following the announcement. The shares of Netscape's CEO, James Barksdale, were estimated by *Newsweek*, in April 1999, to be worth $700 million. Barksdale was quoted as saying of the merger: "This alternative had greater shareholder value."

These developments have had a mixed effect on merger arbitrage specialists. There are more opportunities, but strategic noncompetitive mergers generally lead to smaller arbitrage spreads, although firms with high stock prices have been willing to pay relatively high premiums in order to take advantage of their stock price as ready currency. In hostile takeovers and multiple-bidder situations, buyers tend to be less disciplined and more inclined to overpay for an acquisition.

Stress Period: The Third Quarter of 1998

August of 1998 was the worst single month for merger arbitrage since January of 1990. The strategy showed sub-par returns throughout the summer of 1998. Spreads were chased in because of the overextension of capital into the strategy. Many cross-arbitrage (multistrategy) players had added merger arbitrage positions to their portfolios by using a large amount of leverage. This overextension of capital came to the fore when the Russian debt crisis triggered a liquidity squeeze that dominated all other factors in the market.

The HFRI Merger Arbitrage Index, which included some 28 managers specializing in merger arbitrage with an average fund size of $61 million, showed a −5.69 percent return for the month. This figure, which was poor in its own right, masked even worse performance among cross-arbitrage shops such as Long Term Capital Management (LTCM), which was carrying highly leveraged merger arbitrage positions coming into August, and was forced to sell those equity positions to provide the liquidity necessary to support the less liquid portions of its portfolios, reduce overall leverage, and meet investor demands for redemptions.

The extent to which firms such as LTCM were involved in the merger arbitrage market will never be fully known, but discoveries such as LTCM's 4-million-share position in Ciena–Tellabs indicate that this firm was heavily involved. In addition, the proprietary trading desks of some major sell-side firms closed up their merger arbitrage activity and liquidated all of their positions, in an effort to reduce the overall risk profile of the firm. The liquidity squeeze caused corporate credit spreads (the spread between corporate debt and Treasuries) to blow out, and put pressure on any credit-sensitive deals. In particular, leveraged buyouts suffered because of their dependence on the junk bond market.

Many investors began to fear that the Russian situation, in conjunction with the continued Asian financial crisis and political instability in the United States and abroad, might prompt a world-wide recession. This fear affected the merger arbitrage community in two ways:

1. Deal flow dried up as potential buyers put planned deals on hold until the global economy stabilized.

2. Arbitrageurs began to question whether buyers would follow through with previously announced deals.

Table 7.1 Merger Arbitrage Returns, 1990–1999

Number of Funds	Average Size (Millions of $US)	Year	Jan	Feb	Mar	Apr	May
7	5	1990	−6.46	1.71	2.90	0.98	2.28
8	5	1991	0.01	1.59	2.30	2.83	1.55
8	5	1992	1.96	0.96	1.34	0.14	0.00
10	5	1993	2.12	1.64	0.49	1.30	1.17
11	11	1994	1.50	−0.41	1.37	−0.25	1.22
17	30	1995	0.86	1.45	1.49	0.35	1.26
20	41	1996	1.57	1.29	1.51	1.62	1.46
19	55	1997	1.04	0.39	1.05	−0.70	1.92
28	61	1998	0.96	1.89	1.05	1.59	−0.60
40	72	1999	0.71	0.25	1.05	1.31	2.04

* Annual represents geometric compounded average.

With a perceived increase in event risk and many large players exiting the market to meet liquidity concerns, a huge amount of product was dumped on the market, and merger arbitrage spreads widened dramatically.

During the difficult period between the Russian debt crisis in August and the Federal Reserve's easing of interest rates in October, surprisingly many announced deals that predated the Russian crisis were completed. Other than the Ciena–Tellabs debacle, almost all stock-for-stock deals were completed. Some stock-for-stock mergers with collars became problematic if the buyer traded down through the bottom of the collar. Leveraged buyouts generally were not completed because of their dependence on the junk bond market.

Almost all merger arbitrage managers took a loss in August on a mark-to-market basis. Participants who were forced to sell out of positions, to provide liquidity and meet redemption requests, fared even worse. Managers who were not overleveraged going into this difficult period, and thus were less affected by the liquidity squeeze,

Jun	Jul	Aug	Sep	Oct	Nov	Dec	Annual*
0.73	0.02	−0.82	−4.58	0.73	2.19	1.21	0.44
1.12	1.44	0.64	1.10	1.41	1.38	1.20	17.86
0.30	1.45	0.12	1.34	0.40	−2.22	1.91	7.90
2.25	1.54	1.67	1.85	2.05	0.86	1.65	20.24
0.89	0.68	1.99	0.59	−0.26	−0.22	1.48	8.88
2.47	1.35	1.35	1.63	0.91	2.13	1.31	17.86
0.78	0.81	1.64	0.81	1.23	1.38	1.37	16.61
2.13	1.60	1.04	2.13	0.84	2.02	1.90	15.79
0.50	−0.57	−5.69	1.74	2.14	2.33	1.94	7.23
1.61	1.38	0.52	1.28	0.93	2.37	1.08	15.52

minimized their losses and were able to build positions very cheaply as spreads widened out. Managers who were able to put on positions while spreads were wide reaped the benefits in the fourth quarter, when many of these deals closed.

RETURNS

Merger arbitrage managers recovered nicely in the fourth quarter of 1998 and continued to perform well in 1999. Deal flow for 1999 hit record highs, offering ample opportunities for the strategy. In addition, the proportion of failed deals remained close to the historical average. Historical returns for the strategy are illustrated in Table 7.1 on pages 172–173, and the growth of $1,000 invested in merger arbitrage (as measured by the HFRI Merger Arbitrage Index) in 1990 is shown in Figure 7.1.

Figure 7.1   Merger Arbitrage: Growth of $1,000, January 1990–December 1999

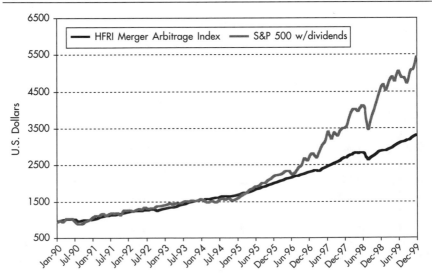

Equity Hedge 8

Equity hedge managers build equity portfolios by combining core long holdings with short sales of stock or stock index options. Their net market exposure (long positions – short positions) varies, depending on the manager's preference and on market conditions. Ideally, they increase long exposure in bull markets and decrease it (or even go net short) in a bear market. The short exposure is often intended to act as a hedge against a general stock market decline, but many managers also hope to generate an ongoing positive return from their short positions.

In a rising market, well-chosen long positions increase in value as fast as or faster than the market, and well-chosen short positions increase less than the long positions, or even decline in value. Similarly, in a declining market, well-chosen short holdings tend to fall more rapidly than the market falls, and well-chosen long holdings fall less rapidly than the market, or even increase in value. Although underperforming short positions reduce returns in a rising market, equity hedge managers accept this reduction in returns in exchange for the protection the short positions can provide in case the market declines.

The source of return for the long side of the portfolio is similar to that of traditional stock pickers. The source of return for the strategy as a whole differs in the use of short selling and hedging to outperform the market in a declining or downward-trending market. Thus, in a bull market, equity hedge managers should achieve positive returns, but smaller returns than if they held only long positions. In a bear market, they may make negative returns but will lose less than if they held only long positions. Therefore, one can expect equity hedge managers to make returns over time that are similar to those of long-only managers but have less volatility.

INVESTMENT THEMES AND FUNDAMENTAL ANALYSIS

Equity hedge approaches incorporate, to a greater or lesser extent, two techniques:

1. Investment themes, which incorporate ideas about macroeconomic trends—broad notions that will affect share valuations in the future.

2. Fundamental analysis, a method of assessing a particular company's financial health and future prospects. The analysis can be subdivided into quantitative and qualitative aspects.

Investment Themes

Most equity hedge managers try to be early in identifying economic trends—sometimes referred to as investment themes—that will have a major impact on the market. Identifying the industries and technologies that will come into demand and remain so is an important part of identifying candidates for long positions.

After identifying the portions of the market to focus on, equity hedge managers look for companies that are well positioned to take advantage of these economic and technological developments. In different industries, the factors that come into play usually vary. For example, Dell Computer Corporation has vaulted to the forefront of the personal computer industry by implementing a direct-sales, build-to-order strategy. A manager who identified the competitive advantage of this innovative sales strategy early would have taken a long position in Dell and benefited from the subsequent rise in its share price.

Another good example involves the debate whether the massive potential of the Internet for voice, data, and video services and products will be delivered to consumers in the future by way of cable-modem or fiber-optic cables—or other media such as satellites. A manager who feels that cable-modems will win out would probably take a long position in telecommunications giant AT&T. AT&T has positioned itself to dominate the cable-modem market by acquiring two of the four largest cable television companies.

These are just two examples of how an equity hedge manager might use macro ideas about the economy to locate good long candidates. Astute managers may look for identifiable catalysts that will focus the investment community's attention on the candidates, such as better-than-expected earnings or positive press releases.

On the short side, equity hedge managers look for the inverse. Short ideas often emerge within the framework of long investment themes when managers attempt to identify good long candidates. While trying to determine what company has a competitive advantage in an area, the manager often finds a competitor that is suffering from a competitive disadvantage such as bad management, accounting difficulties, insufficient cash flow, or excessive debt. Even more than on the long side, managers try to identify a catalyst, such as a negative press release or a poor earnings report, that will accelerate negative sentiment within the investment community.

Investment themes may seem to be a logical part of "growth" investing, but most "value" managers are also making use of macro ideas about where the economy is headed next (these two key investment styles, growth and value, are discussed later in this chapter). Managers who favor value weigh these macro ideas about economic trends against the valuations of the companies that will be affected by them. Companies that are currently out of favor but are positioned to take advantage of an emerging trend are ideal long candidates for equity hedge managers who favor value stocks.

Fundamental Analysis

As it applies to the investment world, fundamental analysis refers to the elementary or essential components of a company that can potentially affect its stock price. Generally, fundamentals can be placed in two categories: quantitative and qualitative.

Quantitative

Quantitative fundamental analysis collects quantifiable statistical indications of a company's financial well-being. Classic examples of such indicators are price-to-earnings ratios and price-to-book-value ratios. Because these statistical indicators are produced uniformly across the entire industry, they help to make to some very different companies readily comparable. Equity hedge managers can arrive at most of the commonly used quantitative fundamentals by examining a company's publicly available financial documents.

Qualitative

Qualitative fundamentals are far more subjective than quantitative ones. For example, it would be difficult to assign an objective measurement to the quality of a company's business plan, but this is an essential factor in the company's success or failure and thus is worthy of attention. Qualitative analysis involves assessing factors that cannot be quantified but are integral to the future success of the company. Examples of these factors include: business plans, quality of management, competitive position, and public sentiment toward the company. Often, qualitative analysis involves projecting the future path of the company.

EQUITY HEDGE APPROACHES

A number of key factors make up an equity hedge strategy, and these factors are essential to distinguishing among different equity hedge managers. The seven most important factors are: (1) quantitative analysis vs. qualitative analysis mix; (2) investment universe; (3) investment style; (4) liquidity; (5) net market exposure; (6) research; and (7) use of leverage. Each of these factors is defined briefly below, and in-depth discussions of investment style, net market exposure, and research follow.

Quantitative vs. Qualitative Mix

Managers value quantitative and qualitative analysis differently. At one end of the spectrum are managers who are highly dependent on quantitative analysis; these managers bear a close resemblance to equity market-neutral and statistical arbitrage managers, and they may rely solely on modeled statistical indications to guide their investment decisions. At the other end of the spectrum are managers who rely on qualitative analysis. They generate their ideas by talking to industry contacts, listening to conference calls, and making on-site company visits. They run the numbers only as a check on what they have discovered "in the field." It is possible to find managers anywhere along this spectrum.

Universe of Stocks

Because managers have a limited capacity to conduct fundamental research, they must concentrate on some segment of the equity market. The screening process may be driven by market capitalization, manager expertise, or particular investment themes. Most managers actively track a relatively small group of companies or ideas and keep a larger group "on the radar screen."

Style

The two major styles of equity investing are *value* and *growth*. At the extremes are managers who solely do one or the other; in between are various mixes of the two. In recent times, the line between the two styles has become blurred. "Value" and "growth" often describe ways of thinking about stocks rather than succinct investment styles.

Value

Value investors buy out-of-favor stocks that are priced cheaply because of low profits or underutilized assets. The manager believes they will perform well in the future, so he or she holds these positions until their underlying strength returns the stock price to expected levels. On the short side, value investors find stocks whose underlying fundamentals do not justify the prices the stocks are fetching, and they sell those stocks short.

Quantitative measures of value assess a company's current capital value and its future earnings prospects. The manager then determines how much investors have to pay to realize this future value. Many of these measures are "bang for your buck," that is, some key measure of value over the stock price:

- Price/Earnings (P/E)—How much do I pay for the company's earnings stream?
- Price/Book Value (P/B)—How much do I pay for the company's assets?
- Price/Sales—How much do I pay for the company's revenues?
- Total Assets/Sales—How much revenue is being generated by assets?
- Discounted Cash Flow
- Dividend Discount Model—Is the current price equal to the present value of all future cash flows?
- Changes in Operating Margins
- Return on Equity—How well is equity utilized?
- Excess Cash Flow—Is the company able to support future earnings and service current debt?
- Dividend Yield—What is the amount of current income generated by the stock?

What is undervalued and what is overvalued? In the past, managers would often have strict P/E or P/B rules for inclusion in their portfolios, such as a P/E ratio of 12 or under. The 1990s' bull market challenged such rules and made value managers think long and hard about revising such rules upward. But although valuations are a hot topic for debate, what constitutes a good value is a moving target that varies by sector and industry. Older, settled industries in which companies have established earnings streams, such as the automobile industry, are generally subject to traditional valuation rules. In newer industries, such as the Internet, where companies are fighting to establish a market presence, the old valuation rules appear now to be more dubious. However, these rules are sure to regain their importance after the initial rush to buy these stocks at any price pushes valuations to levels that are unjustified by the underlying businesses. As has happened in other notable extended bull markets (Japan's stock market of the late 1980s provides a good example), investors who have reaped huge gains from increasing share prices tend to focus on the future and on earnings potential. But when the momentum slows, or even reverses, that emphasis tends to shift to the present and current earnings.

Value Example: Merrill Lynch.   Merrill Lynch & Co. provides investment, financing, insurance, and related services to individuals and institutions on a global basis, through its broker, dealer, banking, insurance, and other financial services subsidiaries. The company has assets of over $300 billion. Table 8.1 shows selected fundamentals for Merrill Lynch for the past five full fiscal years.

At its low in October 1998, Merrill Lynch's stock traded down to 42. Although this corresponded to the downturn in the stock market and to public disclosures by Merrill Lynch about trading losses associated with Russia and the Long Term Capital Management bailout, the company remained an enormous dividend-paying financial entity with a proven stream of cash flows and valuable underlying assets. The drop in the stock

Table 8.1 Merrill Lynch: Selected Fundamentals*

Fiscal Year (Dec. 31)	1994	1995	1996	1997	1998
Revenues ($ millions)	18,233	21,513	25,713	32,499	35,853
Earnings per Share	2.37	2.71	4.08	4.79	3.00
Share Price (12/31)	16.56	24.13	39.29	71.28	66.04
Price/Earnings (12/31)	6.99	8.90	9.63	14.88	22.01

* Source: The Wall Street Journal; wsj.com. Figures are adjusted for stock splits.

price allowed astute value investors to buy Merrill for less than nine times its previous year's earnings and less than two times book value. The stock had consistently traded close to or at twenty times earnings until the third quarter.

This case provides a great example of how value investors think. Value investors ask themselves: What are the company's underlying assets, earnings, and cash flows? What will those factors be worth, going forward? What price will I have to pay to realize these earnings? It is also a good example of how value interacts with macro events and investment themes. If investors had felt that the global financial system was headed for ruin and a long bear market was forthcoming, then Merrill probably would not have represented a value at any price. On the other hand, if investors felt that the third-quarter crisis would soon be remedied and the bull market in the United States would resume, then Merrill Lynch represented an excellent chance to purchase an out-of-favor stock at a bargain price. In addition, longer-term trends in the United States—such as the explosion in retail investing and the increased stock market trading volume, from which Merrill was well positioned to benefit—may have entered into the assessment. Value investors who were able to see beyond the uncertainty caused by the global financial turmoil and determine that Merrill's stock represented a good value when priced in the 40s were rewarded handsomely. The stock traded as high as 92 in March 1999.

Growth

Growth investors buy the stocks of rapidly growing companies whose fundamental business is so strong that the investors feel it justifies almost any valuation. The classic growth stock at this writing is Amazon.com, which has yet to register a profit, but whose innovative Internet retailing business and name recognition have chased its stock price up to heights that cannot begin to be justified by the company's revenues and net income. On the short side, growth investors look for companies that are fundamentally flawed and whose stock price will be carried down by these shortcomings.

Quantitative measures of growth are generally measures of a company's growth potential, as reflected in future earnings and changes in investors' expectations. The usual assumption is that stock prices are driven by investors' expectations, which can be quantified in analysts' earnings estimates. Thus, revisions of these estimates, either up or down, can be a powerful indicator of a company's growth trend. Common growth measures include:

- Earnings Growth—How rapidly are earnings growing?
- Earnings Growth Forward to Price/Earnings—How does the measure of growth relate to the P/E ratio?
- Earnings Estimate Revisions—What changes in expectations are indicated?
  - Consensus among analysts—How much diffusion is there within the analyst community?
  - Change in estimate relative to price
  - Magnitude and direction of changes in individual estimates
  - Likelihood of future revisions
- Earnings Surprises—Do the charts support the expectations for earnings?

Qualitative measures of growth are perhaps more important to this style than quantitative ones. The bottom line for growth investors is whether the company in question will be successful in the future. Thus, this style of investing is sometimes thought of as having a more subjective or qualitative bent than value investing. Qualitative growth factors—business plan, management, competitive position, and the like—are key pieces of information for growth managers to evaluate.

As with value, what constitutes growth differs by industry. It would be illogical to expect traditional cyclical stocks to experience the explosive growth seen recently in information technology stocks. Many managers compare a company with other companies within the same industry to determine how quickly that company is growing.

Growth Example: Cisco Systems. Cisco Systems provides networking solutions that connect computing devices and computer networks. The connections allow people to access or transfer information without regard to differences in time, place, or type of computer system. Throughout the 1990s, Cisco's management used numerous acquisitions and investments in research and development to improve its products and to create new products that would allow it to capture more market share in the rapidly growing computer networking industry. The company foresaw the growth of the Internet and positioned itself to take advantage of the Net's explosive growth. With the emergence of the Internet as a driving force in the economy, Cisco now finds itself in a dominant position within this rapidly growing segment of its industry. As leading international and U.S. service providers have begun to deploy integrated networks based on Internet Protocol (IP) services, Cisco has offered them what it calls "New World Internet communications solutions," based on a single network that integrates voice, data, and video. As a result, the company's sales and

Table 8.2 Cisco Systems: Selected Fundamentals*

Fiscal Year (to July 31)	1993	1994	1995	1996	1997	1998	1999
% Increase in Net Sales	91	92	67	84	57	31	43
% Increase Earnings per Share	75	71	28	94	10	19	32
% Increase Share Price	94	−19	165	86	54	81	95
Price/Earnings at Fiscal Year End	41	19	39	37	52	76	100

* Source: The Wall Street Journal: wsj.com. Figures are adjusted for stock splits.

earnings, depicted in Table 8.2, grew rapidly throughout the 1990s and led many investors to expect that they will continue to do so in the future.

From July 1993 to July 1999, Cisco's share price increased 2,000 percent, and earnings per share increased 785 percent. The company now has a market capitalization of over $200 billion. There is no question that Cisco is well positioned to continue to expand its business, but an investor must ask whether that potential for growth justifies paying 100 times earnings for the stock. From the standpoint of a manager who has taken the expansion of the Internet as an investment theme, the price of the stock may be irrelevant. The important point is that the company will continue to grow rapidly. Growth managers believe that the share price of a rapidly growing company will continue to rise as long as its business continues to expand.

Liquidity

In equity hedge strategies, liquidity is a function of the market capitalization of the companies in the portfolio and the size of the manager's position in each company. Large-capitalization (large-cap) companies whose stocks are actively traded are considered more liquid. In addition, a position in a large-cap company is more liquid than a position of an equal dollar amount in a small-capitalization (small-cap) company because the position represents a smaller percentage of the outstanding shares. The average market capitalization of an equity hedge portfolio serves as an indication of its liquidity.

Net Market Exposure

Net market exposure is a rough indication of a manager's exposure to systematic rises or declines in the overall level of stock prices. Ideally, managers have more exposure in bull markets than in bear markets. A simplified version of the formula commonly used to calculate market exposure is:

$$\text{Market Exposure} = \frac{(\text{Long exposure} - \text{Short exposure})}{\text{Capital}}.$$

For example, a fund manager has $1,000,000 in capital to invest, and borrows an additional $400,000. The manager then takes long positions worth $800,000 and short positions worth $600,000. The manager's net market exposure is $200,000/$1,000,000, or 20 percent net long. Conservative fund managers generally keep market exposure between 0 and 100 percent, or even go net short. More aggressive funds may magnify risk by using leverage to exceed 100 percent exposure.

Some managers adjust net market exposure to reflect a macro view of the direction of the market. For other managers, net market exposure is simply a function of whether they find better investment opportunities on the long side or the short side. These managers take short positions primarily as stand-alone opportunities to make investment returns, rather than as a hedge against market decline. (The position still serves as a hedge, but this is a secondary effect.) This kind of position is sometimes referred to as a trading position, to distinguish it from short positions taken as part of an overall portfolio hedge. Net market exposure is usually an indication of how aggressive or conservative a manager is, but it is important to analyze the nature of the underlying positions to determine whether market exposure is a result of an overall hedge or of trading positions.

Research

Managers must base their investment decisions on their analyses of information about companies. Ideally, this information is accurate and timely, and has some level of predictive power. But because the possible sources of company information are myriad, and vary in quality and perspective, it is important to ask where a manager obtains information. Some of the most important information sources are:

- Trade journals and newspapers—Most managers read *The Wall Street Journal, The Financial Times*, and other more specialized publications, to keep abreast of news and events that may lead to investment ideas.

- Data feeds—Among the various electronic sources of financial information available to managers are: Bloomberg, Reuters, EDGAR Online, and other providers of more specialized information.

- Industry contacts—Managers (or their analysts) build networks of contacts within the financial industry and the various industries that interest them. Some analysts may have formerly worked in a particular industry and can use their expertise to analyze stocks in that industry.

- Conference calls—Many companies schedule conference calls to communicate with a large number of investors and potential investors at one time. Participating in such calls can be a way to gain access to company management, or to become familiar with a company without having to expend the resources needed to make an on-site visit.

- Company visits—Many managers rely on on-site visits and conversations with customers, suppliers, and competitors, to learn details that may not be apparent from a company's publicly available documents and press releases. Site visits also allow managers to get a "hands-on" feel for how the company operates on a day-to-day basis.

- Street research—For assessments of candidate companies, some managers rely on specialized analysts at large Wall Street brokerage houses. Most of these analysts follow a small number of companies or a single industry, and thus, the managers argue, they have a high level of expertise in that particular area. Street research, however, must always be viewed with caution. It is often designed to create brokerage commissions rather than to objectively portray the company in question. The prevalent analyst rating scale is inflated to the extent that sell recommendations are rarely issued.

- Newsletters—The number of industry newsletters available is rapidly increasing.

- Internet sites—The Internet has become a fertile source of information. Company Web pages, news searches, news-groups, and other links have become important data sources, particularly with the advent of electronic brokerage. In addition, many financial publications are now offered online with searchable archives.

Leverage

Most equity hedge strategists use leverage, which allows a manager to invest more than the amount of contributed capital by borrowing funds. Leverage increases risk, but allows managers to add new stocks to their portfolio without having to sell another stock first. Aggressive equity hedge managers use leverage to move quickly, in order to exploit investment opportunities. Although conservative equity hedge managers use leverage more sparingly, the deployment of some amount of leverage is a standard characteristic of equity hedge funds.

RISKS AND RISK CONTROL

Stock-Picking Risk

When manages pick a stock for the long or short side of their portfolio, they take on risks specific to that company. These risks include, but are not limited to: regulatory issues, threats to market share or proprietary position, decreasing profit margins and other significant industry trends, continuity of management, dilution of current business due to future expansion, emergence of new technologies, and a possibility that the company will be involved in a merger or acquisition. Company-specific risks are inevitable, but a manager should be able to say with conviction that these risks are acceptable, given the potential for the share price to increase (for long positions) or decrease (for short positions). The essential tool for managing these risks is in-depth fundamental research and analysis that allow managers to make predictions about the future based on all the currently available information.

In addition, equity hedge managers may counter specific risks with short, specific hedging positions. For example, a manager might hedge against exposure to a specific industry by pair trading. A manager who trades in pairs takes a long position in a company with a favorable outlook in a particular industry, and a corresponding short position in another company in the same industry (often a competitor). If a systemic drop occurs in the prices of the industry as a whole (e.g., bad news for a large company in an industry is often taken as indicative of the entire industry), the long and short positions will offset each other.

Market Risk

The stock market as a whole is vulnerable to changes in the financial community or in the overall economy that can affect all companies and, thus, can cause directional changes in the overall level of stock prices. Interest rates are a good example of a directional change. An easy monetary policy (lower interest rates) usually causes share prices to increase because of the liquidity it creates. Conversely, a monetary tightening (higher interest rates), which is usually intended to keep inflation in check, reduces liquidity by raising the cost of money. Bond markets then become more attractive to investors, and share prices fall.

Equity hedge managers can mitigate the risk of systemic changes in stock prices by monitoring macro factors relative to stock market valuations, and by carefully adjusting their long and short exposures as the market dictates. This process is by nature imperfect, but many managers attempt to avoid getting caught too net long in a market decline or too net short in a market rally. The portion of an equity hedge portfolio that is "within the hedge" may approximate market neutrality, but, at any given time, managers can lose money on both their long and short positions. The portion of the portfolio that is not hedged is, of course, susceptible to all the directional caprices of the market.

Universe of Stocks

It is widely held that the stocks of larger, more readily tradable companies trade differently than those of smaller, less liquid companies. More information is available about large companies and large-cap stocks than about smaller companies and their small-cap stocks.

The more information that is available, and the more analysts at big brokerage houses who follow the company, the less likely it is that a single manager will have an informational advantage over other investors. The market for large-cap stocks is thus said to be more efficient than the market for small-cap stocks. Managers must weigh the informational disadvantage associated with large-cap stocks against the gain to be had from liquidity. In addition, a risk is associated with the size of a position relative to the total market capitalization of a company. As mentioned earlier, a position in a large-cap company is more liquid than a position of an equal dollar amount in a small-cap company because the position represents a smaller percentage of the outstanding shares. The average market capitalization of an equity hedge portfolio is an indication of its liquidity.

Managers looking for undiscovered stock stories tend to focus on middle- and small-cap stocks. Generally speaking, the smaller the capitalization, the riskier the stock. Small-cap stocks are often unknown companies that have unproven earnings streams and do not pay dividends. As evidenced in the fall of 1998, small-cap stocks are more adversely affected by a liquidity squeeze. The Russell 2000 index of small-cap stocks lost more than 33 percent from its peak in July 1998 to its trough in October 1998. In spite of 19.62 percent returns in 1999, the index was still only 9.76 percent above its 1998 low. On the other hand, the S&P 500, which lost 19 percent from peak to trough, was up 27.92 percent from its July 1998 level through the end of 1999.

Diversification

Modern portfolio theory has shown that, everything else being equal, a diversified portfolio of stocks experiences less volatility than a concentrated one. This theory is an extension of the old adage, "Don't put all your eggs in one basket." Ideally, in a portfolio of stocks with low correlation, when one position is dropping, another one is gaining and is therefore reducing the volatility of the overall portfolio. Most equity hedge managers also diversify their portfolios across industries and sectors to ensure that happenings in any one sector or industry do not have too much effect on the portfolio as a whole. Many equity hedge strategists use position limits to control the impact any one position can have on the portfolio as a whole, and to ensure that a particular level of diversification is always present in the portfolio. If a position grows in market value and thus achieves a larger-than-intended weighting in the portfolio, the manager may trim that position back.

Sell Disciplines

Many managers determine a target valuation for a stock and then purchase it based on what they think it should be worth. When the stock reaches the target value, they either sell the position or reassess the estimated value. Managers may sell the stock before it reaches its target value, if new information causes them to distrust the underlying growth or value qualities that originally prompted the purchase. When the price of a stock does not behave as expected, the manager reassesses the position. Generally, equity hedge managers are more tolerant of unexpected price moves in core long-term holdings than in trading positions.

Leverage

Most equity hedge strategists use some amount of leverage. Leverage allows managers to add new stocks to a portfolio without having to wait until they can sell another stock. Alternatively, managers may use leverage to increase the size of favored positions. Aggressive equity hedge managers use leverage to move quickly and exploit investment opportunities. More conservative equity hedge managers use leverage more sparingly, but the deployment of some amount of leverage is a characteristic of equity hedge funds in general.

SOURCE OF RETURN

The prices of individual stocks can, and often do, move in response to company-specific factors that are unrelated to the macro movements of the overall stock market. Thus, an equity hedge manager derives returns, to some extent, from an ability to pick stocks that will outperform or underperform the market. On the long side, this is no different from traditional long-only managers. The strategy differs in the use of short positions to derive returns from the manager's ability to identify fundamentally flawed or overvalued companies whose stock prices will fall in the future.

Theoretically, an equity hedge strategy allows managers to make money in both up and down markets because they retain the flexibility to go both long and short. In practice, short positions often reduce returns in up markets. Equity hedge portfolios may not outperform a traditional long-only stock portfolio in a bull market, but, over time, they should outperform the stock market on a risk-adjusted basis because short positions allow the strategy to significantly outperform the stock market in down or sideways markets.

Picking individual stocks is an important source, but not the only source, of return for equity hedge managers. Another key source of return is derived from the *relationship between stocks in the portfolio,*—in particular, the relationship of long positions to short positions. Just as constructing a portfolio of correlated stocks dilutes the volatility-reducing gains from diversification, hedging for the sake of hedging dilutes the effectiveness of the technique and may end up being nothing more than a drag on returns. Constructing hedges that target specific risks involves very careful attention to the relationships between the contents of the portfolio. At the portfolio level, equity managers can mitigate market risk, and profit from declining markets, by adjusting net market exposure. For individual positions, industry-specific risks can be hedged by shorting another company in the industry. Needless to say, balancing hedging objectives for the overall portfolio with company- or industry-specific hedges is more an art than a science.

RECENT GROWTH AND DEVELOPMENTS IN EQUITY HEDGE INVESTING

Equity hedge as a strategy has grown from 5 percent of hedge fund assets in 1990 to over 11 percent in 1999. Record growth in the equity markets and the outstanding performance of the equity hedge strategy have fueled the dramatic growth during this period. Equity hedge managers, as measured by the HFRI Equity Hedge Index, have produced returns comparable to the S&P 500 at a much lower level of volatility. The strategy is appealing to investors who worry that the current level of valuations in the equity market is untenable and, in turn, seek the protection of a hedged equity portfolio.

The third and fourth quarters of 1998 provided a good example of how the equity hedge strategy performs in an environment that is very difficult for traditional long-only managers. Many equity hedge managers registered negative returns during the third quarter of 1998, but the short component of their portfolios cushioned the fall. The HFRI Equity Hedge Index returned –7.65 percent in August 1998, while the S&P 500 dropped over 14.5 percent and the Russell 2000 Small-Cap Index was down over 19 percent.

The market bottomed out in the first week of October as concerns about liquidity and global financial stability peaked. Subsequently, the Japanese pushed through a banking bill, and the Federal Reserve cut interest rates for a second time in a three-week span, thereby restoring liquidity and confidence to the U.S. market.

Led by large-cap issues, technology stocks, and financial stocks, U.S. stocks staged a rally during which they recovered most of what they had lost, and, in some cases, pushed into positive territory.

In 1998, the HFRI Equity Hedge Index showed returns of 2.47 percent in October, 3.84 percent in November, and 5.39 percent in December, compared with 8.13 percent, 6.06 percent, and 5.76 percent in the same periods for the S&P 500. The strategy performed as one would expect during the period: outperforming the market during the correction, and underperforming the market during the momentum-driven rally that followed. Figure 8.1 shows the percentage change in selected U.S. stock indexes during the period.

Underlying this performance were key developments in the U.S. equity markets that affected all equity hedge managers, although to different degrees. Managers were forced to interpret these developments and assess the effect they would have on their

Figure 8.1   Selected U.S. Stock Indexes, July 1, 1998 to December 31, 1998

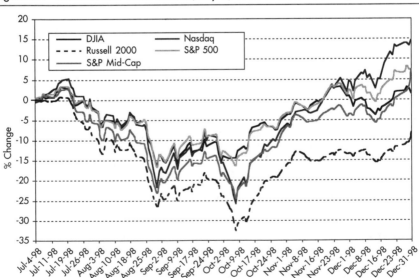

portfolios, the risks they presented, and how to manage those risks. The three most notable trends during this period were: (1) the out-performance of large-cap stocks, compared to small-cap and mid-cap stocks; (2) the higher volatility (on both the down side and the up side) exhibited by the technology-rich Nasdaq Composite Index, when compared with the Dow Jones Industrial Average and the S&P 500; and (3) the outperformance of growth stocks versus value stocks.

The miserable performance of small-cap stocks during this period can be attributed to the flight to quality that was initiated by Russia's partial default on its internal debt and furthered by the near-failure of Long Term Capital Management. The uncertainty about global financial stability created by these events, as well as concerns about sagging corporate earnings and a possible reces-sion, made investors more willing to pay a liquidity premium for large-cap stocks that would trade even in a bear market. For exam-ple, an investor holding a position in IBM is more likely to find a buyer during a crisis than an investor holding a position in a small technology start-up firm. As noted previously, small-cap stocks are generally deemed more risky than large-cap stocks; thus, in a period when risk management becomes paramount, small-cap stocks sell off more than large-cap stocks.

From its peak on July 16 to its trough on October 8, the Russell 2000 index of small-cap stocks lost over 33 percent. By contrast, the Dow Jones Industrials lost about 18 percent from peak to trough, and the S&P 500 lost nearly 20 percent. Small-cap stocks did not participate proportionately in the fourth-quarter rebound either. The S&P 500 ended the six months from July 1 to December 31 up over 7 percent; the Russell 2000 was down almost 8 percent for the same period. Equity hedge managers who were able to mitigate ex-posure to this liquidity risk, whether by diversifying across market capitalization or by balancing long positions in small-cap stocks with short positions in other small-cap issues, performed better than those who did not adjust their portfolio to reflect the developments of this period.

The second pair of trends are linked. The Nasdaq Composite Index contained many of the period's favorite growth or momentum stocks, and had become almost synonymous with growth and momentum. Investors' preference for growth stocks became pronounced in May 1998, and, with only short lapses triggered by profit taking and financial crises, remained so through the end of 1999. This long-term trend was put on hold in 1998 as liquidity became the overriding concern from late August through the middle of October. The Nasdaq Composite Index dropped over 30 percent from peak to trough, as compared with 18 percent for the Dow Jones Industrials and 20 percent for the S&P 500. During the rebound, however, it ran past the other two indexes. By the end of the year, the Nasdaq had gained 40 percent over its low point less than three months earlier. It followed this rebound by gaining an astounding 84 percent in 1999.

Table 8.3   Equity Hedge Fund Returns, 1990–1999

Number of Funds	Average Size (Millions of $US)	Year	Jan	Feb	Mar	Apr	May
12	44	1990	−3.34	2.85	5.67	−0.87	5.92
26	48	1991	4.90	5.20	7.22	0.47	3.20
37	33	1992	2.49	2.90	−0.28	0.27	0.85
59	29	1993	2.09	−0.57	3.26	1.30	2.72
78	42	1994	2.35	−0.40	−2.08	−0.37	0.41
90	41	1995	0.30	1.68	2.09	2.64	1.22
102	70	1996	1.06	2.82	1.90	5.34	3.70
133	76	1997	2.78	−0.24	−0.73	−0.27	5.04
210	100	1998	−0.16	4.09	4.54	1.39	−1.27
226	122	1999	4.98	−2.41	4.05	5.25	1.22

* Annual represents geometric compounded average.

To some extent, investors' emphasis on growth investing, at the expense of value investing, is part of a natural style rotation. Investors who have reaped huge gains from increasing share prices (as an increasing number of U.S. investors have, in the 1990s' bull market) tend to focus on the future and earnings potential. When the momentum slows or even reverses, however, that emphasis tends to shift to the present and current earnings. It remains to be seen whether the new generation of retail investors and the explosion of financial technology and available data have changed this relationship. In any case, traditional long-only managers who bought Nasdaq stocks during the second half of 1998 may have made large momentum-driven returns, depending on their timing, but those returns came at a cost of extreme volatility. Equity hedge managers who bought similar stocks and hedged them properly with short positions to eliminate an implicit style bet were able to participate in these returns to an extent, while dampening the whipsaw volatility.

Jun	Jul	Aug	Sep	Oct	Nov	Dec	Annual*
2.52	2.00	−1.88	1.65	0.77	−2.29	1.02	14.43
.59	1.41	2.17	4.30	1.16	−1.08	5.02	40.15
−0.92	2.76	−0.85	2.51	2.03	4.51	3.38	21.32
3.01	2.12	3.84	2.52	3.11	−1.93	3.59	27.94
−0.41	0.91	1.27	1.32	0.40	−1.48	0.74	2.61
4.73	4.46	2.93	2.90	−1.44	3.43	2.56	31.04
−0.73	−2.87	2.63	2.18	1.56	1.66	0.83	21.75
1.97	5.05	1.35	5.69	0.39	−0.93	1.42	23.05
0.50	−0.67	−7.65	3.16	2.47	3.84	5.39	15.98
3.80	0.61	0.04	0.45	2.74	7.23	11.30	46.14

Figure 8.2 Equity Hedge: Growth of $1,000, January 1990–December 1999

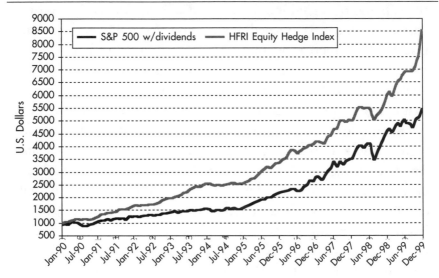

In 1999, the U.S. equities resumed their upward path. As mentioned previously, the Nasdaq Composite Index was up 84 percent for the year, and all other indexes registered significant gains as well. Equity hedge managers participated in these gains to a large extent; managers included in the HFRI index gained 46.14 percent. This performance continued the stellar returns for equity hedge strategies throughout the 1990s, as shown in Table 8.3 on pages 198–199 and Figure 8.2.

Equity Market-Neutral and Statistical Arbitrage *9*

Equity market-neutral managers strive to generate consistent returns in both up and down markets by selecting positions with a total net exposure of zero. They hold a large number of long equity positions and an equal, or close to equal, dollar amount of offsetting short positions, for a total net exposure close to zero. A zero net exposure, referred to as "dollar neutrality," is a common characteristic of all equity market-neutral managers. By taking long and short positions in equal amounts, the equity market-neutral manager seeks to neutralize the effect that a systemic change would have on values of the stock market as a whole.

Some, but not all, equity market-neutral managers extend the concept of neutrality to risk factors or characteristics such as beta, industry, sector, investment style, and market capitalization. In all equity market-neutral portfolios, stocks expected to outperform the market are held long, and stocks expected to underperform the market are sold short. Returns are derived from the long–short spread, or the amount by which long positions outperform short positions. Thus, equity market-neutral managers, in theory, are able to achieve stable returns, regardless of the overall direction of the stock market.

Some detractors of this strategy refer to equity market-neutral investing as "black box" investing. The proverbial black box is a quantitative computer-based model. Many, but not all, equity market-neutral managers rely on multifactor models to rank stocks relative to one another according to expected returns and exposure to risk factors. Well-constructed quantitative models consolidate large quantities of information about a company into an ordinal ranking that can be compared to a large number of other stocks. In comparison, managers who construct an equity market-neutral portfolio without the aid of a quantitative model are constrained by the amount of time and resources they have available to analyze and track stocks.

It is no coincidence that equity market-neutral investing emerged as a prominent strategy in the 1990s. The philosophical ideas that underlie the strategy have been in circulation for at least fifty years, but, in the past decade, the rapid advances in information technology and financial data availability have made the strategy more practical to implement. The cost of building the necessary infrastructure to analyze thousands of stocks and monitor hundreds of positions has been drastically reduced, allowing small, boutique money management firms to implement the strategy.

Most equity market-neutral managers are highly dependent on quantitative models, but it should be emphasized that a whole spectrum of approaches can be used. They range from qualitative fundamental stock picking, which is quite similar to equity hedge management, to statistical arbitrage, which involves a minimum of human input. Equity statistical arbitrage can be considered a sub-strategy of the equity market-neutral strategy. As with equity market neutral, equity statistical arbitrage managers construct portfolios consisting of equal dollar amounts of equities held long and short. However, there are distinctions between these two strategies. At a general level, the amount of manager discretion involved in statistical arbitrage strategies is far less than in equity market-neutral strategies.

Different managers allow for different amounts of human discretion, but even among the most quantitatively oriented managers, art is involved in building and refining models and in the constant process of review that is required to keep the model dynamic and accurate. The different strategic approaches of equity market-neutral managers and statistical arbitrage managers all involve equal dollar amounts of stocks on the long and short sides, to protect the portfolio from systemic, directional moves in the prices of the stocks. Individual managers can achieve this goal in many different ways.

EQUITY MARKET-NEUTRAL APPROACHES

There are generally three main steps in the equity market-neutral investment process: (1) the initial screen, (2) stock selection, and (3) portfolio construction. Portfolio construction is described in the "Risks and Risk Control" section of this chapter, but it is important to note that this step is not simply a check on stock selection. Rather, it is an interaction with stock selection to produce a portfolio that maximizes expected returns while optimizing risk exposures.

Initial Screen: Universe of Investable Stocks

Managers use models to eliminate stocks that would be difficult to trade in large blocks. Out of a possible 8,000 stocks traded on U.S.

exchanges, the manager winnows the group down to a more manageable number (400 to 2,000), using particular criteria. The most common criteria are: liquidity, ability to short the stock, potential impact on market price, involvement in mergers and acquisitions, and excluded sectors or industries.

Liquidity

The universe of investable stocks is usually, but not always, made up of large, very liquid companies because smaller, less liquid stocks are not always available to borrow and sell short. Market-neutral portfolios often experience high turnover, so it behooves managers to trade stocks that are readily available to borrow and easy to sell. A small number of managers build small- and middle-capitalization equity market-neutral portfolios, but the size of such portfolios is limited. For the most part, equity market-neutral managers limit their universes to the 1,000 or 2,000 most liquid domestic stocks.

Also related to market capitalization is the number of Wall Street analysts who follow a firm. Generally, the larger the firm, the more analysts who follow it. Most managers agree that increased analyst coverage results in more efficient pricing for the largest stocks. Some equity market-neutral managers avoid such efficiently priced stocks by screening out the largest names, or, more commonly, by using a different factor model to analyze the largest names.

Ability to Short

Equity market-neutral managers must be able to sell stocks short. They often eliminate from consideration stocks included on brokers' "hard-to-borrow" lists. Shorting stocks can also present logistical difficulties because of the uptick rule that short sales can be executed only after an upward movement in the stock price. Thus, managers often implement the short side of their portfolio before the long side, so that they do not end up with long positions that they cannot match with short positions.

Market Impact

Equity market-neutral managers who are moving large amounts of stock attempt to measure the impact their purchases will have on the market price of the security. If the purchase of a large block of a certain stock would adversely affect the market price of that stock, then the manager may eliminate that stock from his or her universe of investable stocks. Some managers measure this as a percentage of average daily trading volume. Others calculate how long it would take them to liquidate a particular size position.

Stocks Involved in Mergers and Acquisitions

Many equity market-neutral managers eliminate from consideration any stocks involved in mergers and acquisitions, because the pending merger may affect the stock's price in a way that confounds the ranking assigned to it by the manager's stock selection model. The price of a stock that would normally rank well may be held down by the uncertainty of the outcome of a pending merger. Managers prefer to apply their models to stocks for which they have the most predictive power; therefore, merger stocks may be eliminated.

Excluded Sectors and Industries

Some managers may exclude particular industries or sectors that they believe behave differently or for which their model has less predictive power. For example, managers who heavily weighted traditional measures of value in their models might exclude Internet stocks from their investment universe because traditional measures of value have little or no predictive power for that group of stocks. For the same reason, some managers use sector-specific models with greater predictive value for certain stocks.

Stock Selection

Once managers limit their investment universe, they can begin choosing individual stocks for their portfolio. The second component of equity market-neutral investing in which market-neutral managers can add value is their stock selection models. Philosophically, managers are looking for quantifiable inputs that are indicative of investor behavior. For the most part, the result is a multifactor model that ranks stocks relative to one another on the basis of expected return. Building an effective model involves choosing factors that will have predictive value over a broad range of stocks, and combining scores on each factor into a composite ranking that has a meaningful predictive value.

Technical and Price Momentum Factors

Technical factors generally measure a stock's price momentum as it relates to investors' reactions. Most investors tend to overreact to both good upside news and bad downside news. Price momentum factors reflect some investors' belief that recent price movements may help predict future price movements (perhaps a strange perversion of the tendency of a body in motion to stay in motion). Examples of technical and price momentum factors include:

- Volume on uptick relative to volume on downtick.
- DAIS Static Relative Strength—price relative to market.
- One-Month Relative Strength—four-week change in price relative to the market as a whole.

- Six-Month Relative Strength Value.
- Moving Average Price.

Fundamental Factors—Quantitative

Value Factors.   Value factors seek to emulate the behavior of fundamental value investors. The measures assess a company's current capital value, historical earnings stream, and future earnings prospects, and then determine how much investors have to pay to attain this "value." Many of these measures are "bang for your buck"—that is, some key measure of value over the stock price:

- Price/Earnings—price of current earnings.
- Price/Book Value—price of current capital.
- Price/Cash Flow.
- Discounted Cash Flow.
- Dividend Discount Model—the current price as equal to the present value of all future cash flows.
- Price/Sales—price of current revenues.
- Total Assets over Sales.
- Changes in Operating Margins.
- Earnings Relative to Industry over Price.
- Return on Equity—how well equity is utilized.
- Excess Cash Flow—ability to support future earnings and current debt.
- Dividend Yield—amount of current income generated by the stock.

Growth Factors.   Growth factors are measures of a company's growth potential, as reflected in future earnings and changes in investor expectations. The usual assumption is that stock prices are driven by investor expectations, which can be quantified in analysts' earnings estimates. Thus, revisions of these estimates, either up or down, can be a powerful indicator of a company's growth trend. The following are common measures of growth:

- Earnings Growth.
- Earnings Growth Forward to P/E.
- Earnings Estimate Revisions—changes in expectations:
  - —Consensus among analysts—how much agreement or disagreement exists among analysts.
  - —Change in estimate relative to price.
  - —Magnitude and direction of changes in individual estimates.
  - —Likelihood of future revisions.
- Earnings Surprises—earnings relative to expectations.
- Current Return on Equity vs. Five-Year Range.

Fundamental Factors—Qualitative

Many equity market-neutral managers do not have a qualitative component to their models, but some make use of qualitative data in addition to quantitative data. This information might include data gathered through industry contacts or conversations with company management. In general, this kind of qualitative information is used as an overlay, or check, on model results. The complete lack of qualitative elements is the distinguishing factor between statistical arbitrage and the more general category of equity market neutral. Statistical arbitrage managers seek to eliminate the human element by depending completely on their quantitative models.

Corporate Signals

Equity market-neutral managers are also wary of sudden moves made by employee owners of company stock. These sudden moves may include buybacks and inside trading, which may indicate that public announcements of important information are forthcoming. There is no way for managers to account for this type of information in their models.

Putting It All Together: Creating Relative Rankings

The general form of most multifactor stock selection models is a linear equation of n terms that takes the form:

$$r = \beta_1 f_1 + \beta_2 f_2 + \ldots + \beta_n f_n,$$

where r is a measure of expected return for a stock, and ß (Beta) is the sensitivity of the expected return to changes in the value of its corresponding factor, f. Conventional multifactor models typically use regression analysis to construct a predictive formula linking the values of each of the chosen factors for each stock with that stock's subsequent return. Thus, particular factors are assigned weightings in the equation, based on their estimated predictive value. The regression coefficients for each of the independent variables usually become the factor weights in the multifactor stock-ranking model.

Figure 9.1 illustrates the structure of a hypothetical four-factor model where

$$\beta_a = .4 \ \beta_b = .3 \ \beta_c = .2 \text{ and } \beta_d = .1.$$

The first step is to analyze every stock on each of these individual factors and assign a factor ranking from 1 to 10 (1 = best, 10 = worst). For example, applying these four factor measures to XYZ Corp. might show that its stock has a rank of 1 for Factor A, 6 for Factor B, 2 for Factor C, and 10 for Factor D. Our simple model would then evaluate XYZ Corp. as $(.4 \times 1) + (.3 \times 6) + (.2 \times 2) + (.1 \times 10) = 3.6$, giving XYZ Corp. a score of 3.6 on the multifactor model. After going through the same process for

Figure 9.1   Hypothetical Four-Factor Model

Multifactor Models $r = B_1f_1 + B_2f_2 + ... + B_kf_k$

◆ Step 1. Rank stock on each factor f_i
(ranging from 1–10)
  – *e.g.* XYZ Corp:
  – A = 1, B = 6, C = 2, D = 10

◆ Step 2. Simulations determine
factor weights, compute raw score
  – (.4 x 1) + (.3 x 6) +
  (.2 x 2) + (.1 x 10) = 3.6

◆ Step 3. Sort stocks by raw score and
assign decile rank:
  – 1 = most attractive
  – 10 = least attractive

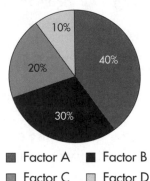

Hypothetical Model

■ Factor A   ■ Factor B
■ Factor C   ■ Factor D

every stock, the model would sort the stocks according to their computed scores and assign them decile (10 percent of the universe) rankings from 1 (most attractive) to 10 (least attractive).

The entire method by which stocks are ranked is summarized in Figure 9.2.

Buy and Sell Rules

Buy and sell decisions are usually functions of the relative ranking system. Stocks held long are usually added to the portfolio when they achieve a certain ranking in the stock selection model and satisfy the risk parameters set for the portfolio as a whole. They are sold when their ranking drops below a certain point. On the short side, stocks ranked below a certain level are sold short and covered when they rise above a particular ranking. Some managers may have more absolute targets for stocks. Buy and sell rules generally

Figure 9.2 Stock Ranking Methodology

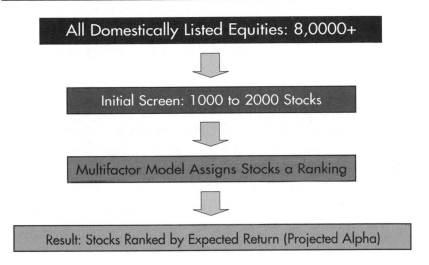

work within the framework of risk optimization; therefore, a buy or sell rule might be violated in order to maintain proper portfolio balance. Indeed, the third key element of the equity market-neutral strategy is proper portfolio construction.

Mean Reversion-Based Approaches

Some statistical arbitrageurs select their stocks via a different method that is based on mean reversion (a statistical anomaly). Managers utilizing mean reversion strategies work under the assumption that anomalies among stock valuations may occur in the short term, but, in the long term, these anomalies will correct themselves as the market processes information. Thus, in a group of stocks that historically trades similarly, short-term events and the tendency of investors to overreact to unexpected news can create pricing disparities (that is, stocks are over- and undervalued relative to the group) that should not hold in the long term. When one stock's statistical price anomaly reverts back to the mean price of its group of stocks, the move is known as *mean reversion*, a common discrepancy exploited by statistical arbitrageurs. The strategy tries to take advantage of related securities whose prices have diverged from their historical norms.

Managers who use mean-reversion-based strategies search for groups of stocks for which the values, over the long term, are positively correlated. Usually, a common theme within each group links the individual equities together. A sector, an industry, or a particular risk factor may define a group. In addition, most managers look for negative correlation with other groups.

As displayed in Figure 9.3, the long-term trend line for the group is relatively smooth, but the short-term individual stock lines are full of peaks and valleys. Mean reversion managers try to sell short the stocks in the group that are at their peaks and buy those that have bottomed out.

Figure 9.3 Stock Groups: Mean Reversion Simplified

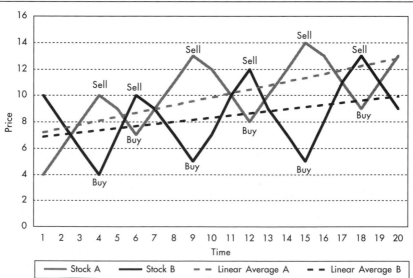

Many mean reversion managers use a relative value system to determine buy and sell decisions. Stocks sold short are usually added to the portfolio when their prices are sufficiently higher than the rest of the group. They are covered when their price drops back closer to the mean of the group. On the long side, stocks that are valued below a certain level are held long until they rise above the mean of the group. Other managers may have more absolute targets for stocks. How managers choose to set up their rules determines how much trading they do, how much turnover the portfolio experiences, and what their transaction costs are. Transaction costs and trade impact on market price are often included in mean reversion models, allowing managers to forgo trade opportunities when the cost of completing the transaction is greater than the potential gain.

Buy and sell rules usually work within the framework of risk–return optimization. Exceptions include stocks that are involved in announced mergers or in other corporate events.

Because markets are ever changing, the factors that unified a group in the past may not always continue to do so. Statistical arbitrage managers must determine when and if to drop stocks from their groups and/or add new ones. For example, in the flight-to-quality situation of the third quarter of 1998, market capitalization and credit quality became such powerful drivers in the market that they could confound formerly effective themes. If the goal is to create a model based on coherent groups with unifying themes, then keeping a model dynamic requires a certain level of vigilance. Deciding which factors are driving which groups, the essential component of model building, is a skill required of the individual manager.

By buying the relatively undervalued stocks in the group and selling short the relatively overvalued stocks in the same group, a manager achieves the dual objectives of buying the stocks with the highest expected returns and selling the stocks with the lowest expected returns, while minimizing net exposure to a group of stocks that share a particular driver. Some examples of stock groups follow:

1. *Sector.* Stocks within a sector often move together. The fortunes of one in the group affect the outlook for the sector as a whole. Thus, statistical arbitrage managers may avoid making sector bets by being long and short equal amounts within a sector.

2. *Industry.* Stocks within an industry often move together. The fortunes of one in the group affect the outlook for the whole group (e.g., a bad earnings report for Compaq affects Dell and Gateway as well). Thus, statistical arbitrage managers may avoid industry bets by being long and short equal amounts within the industry. The bet becomes whether the longs are better than the shorts, rather than whether the industry as a whole will move in a particular direction.

3. *Market capitalization.* In liquidity-driven markets, the prices of large liquid stocks will do better than those of smaller, less liquid stocks. Alternatively, in some market cycles, large-cap stocks become overvalued relative to small-cap stocks, and the small caps may be up while the large caps are flat. In any case, stocks of similar capitalization are subject to systematic directional price moves.

4. *Interest rates.* Companies that are sensitive to interest rate changes include those that are highly leveraged (i.e., those that pay a lot of interest) and those that are big lenders (i.e., those that receive a lot of interest income). The stock prices of these companies may show a correlation to changes in interest rates.

5. *Oil prices.* Companies that are dependent on oil (such as airlines) may be sensitive to changes in oil prices. The

stock prices of these companies may show a correlation to changes in oil prices.

6. *Labor.* Companies with large labor forces, particularly large union labor forces, are subject to disruption by labor strikes. Statistical arbitrage managers may try to neutralize this risk by being long and short equal amounts of such companies.

RISKS AND RISK CONTROL

Portfolio Construction and Optimization

The goal of portfolio construction is to balance reward and risk. After evaluating the defined universe of stocks for both expected return and risk, the market-neutral manager creates the optimal bundle of equal amounts of high-ranked and low-ranked stocks while maintaining, as close as possible, a net zero exposure to the chosen systematic risk factors. Many equity market-neutral managers utilize sophisticated computations known as quadratic optimizers in this process. Common optimizers include APT and BARRA, and many managers have developed their own proprietary optimizer. The reduction of risk associated with neutralizing systematic risk factors must always be weighed against forgone returns. Depending on his or her assessment of the magnitude of the risk and the possible returns, a manager might (1) violate a buy or sell rule in order to maintain proper portfolio balance or (2) allow risk factor exposures to stray from neutrality.

Risk Factors

At the most general level, equity market-neutral managers go long and short equal dollar amounts of equities to insulate their portfolios from unexpected directional moves that affect stocks as an asset class. Some managers extend this logic to other, more specific, systemic risk factors. The logic is the same: By balancing long and short exposure to a risk factor, the risk factor can be theoretically neutralized. The optimization process involves balancing the dual objectives of buying the stocks with the highest expected returns and selling the stocks with the lowest expected returns, while minimizing net exposure to selected risk factors. Some common risk factors are:

1. *Beta.* A measure of the sensitivity of the price of a specific stock, or portfolio of stocks, to changes in the price of the stock market (as measured by the S&P 500). Thus, a Beta-neutral portfolio should be relatively insensitive to stock market swings.

2. *Sector.* Because stocks within a sector often move together, the fortunes of one stock in the group affects the outlook for the sector as a whole. Thus, equity market-neutral managers may avoid sector bets by being long and short equal amounts within the same sector.

3. *Industry.* Similar to sectors, stocks within an industry often move together (e.g., a bad earnings report for Compaq affects Dell and Gateway as well). Thus, equity market-neutral managers may avoid industry bets by being long and short equal amounts within the same industry. The bet becomes whether the longs are better than the shorts, rather than whether the industry as a whole will move in a particular direction.

4. *Market capitalization.* In liquidity-driven markets, the prices of large liquid companies do better than those of smaller, less liquid companies. Alternatively, in some market cycles, large-cap stocks become overvalued relative to small-cap stocks, and small-cap stocks may be up while

large-cap stocks are flat or down. In any case, stocks of similar capitalization are subject to systemic directional price moves driven by liquidity preferences or changes in investor sentiment; therefore, equity market-neutral managers may try to eliminate capitalization bets.

5. *Interest rates.* Companies that are sensitive to interest rate changes include those that are highly leveraged (i.e., those that pay a lot of interest) and those that are big lenders (i.e., those that receive a lot of interest income). The stock prices of these companies may show a correlation to changes in interest rates. Thus, equity market-neutral managers may try to eliminate interest rate bets from their portfolios.

6. *Commodity prices.* Companies that are dependent on oil (airlines) or on another such commodity may be sensitive to changes in the prices of that commodity. The stock prices of these companies may show a correlation to changes in prices of the essential commodity. Therefore, equity market-neutral managers may try to eliminate commodity price bets from their portfolios.

7. *Labor.* Companies with large labor forces, particularly large union labor forces, are subject to disruption by labor strikes. Equity market-neutral managers may try to neutralize this risk by being long and short equal amounts of such companies.

8. *Transaction costs.* The cost of executing a trade is often incorporated in the risk-factor optimization process.

9. *Market impact.* A change in a stock's market price, created by executing a trade, is often incorporated in the risk-factor optimization process.

10. *Price/Earnings.* An equity market-neutral manager may try to eliminate implicit P/E bets.

11. *Price/Book value.* An equity market-neutral manager may try to eliminate implicit P/B bets.

Optimization

After evaluating the defined universe of stocks for expected return (sometimes referred to as projected alpha), most market-neutral managers utilize an optimizer to create a bundle of high-ranked and low-ranked stocks. In doing so, these managers attempt to maximize expected return while maintaining, as closely as possible, a net zero exposure to the chosen systemic risk factors. As previously mentioned, common optimizers include APT and BARRA, and some managers have developed their own proprietary optimizers. Many managers optimize their portfolio on a daily basis, to oversee risk exposures, but most managers rebalance the portfolio only on a weekly or monthly basis, to avoid the transaction costs that they would incur if they were to rebalance the portfolio daily.

Execution and Trading

After the model produces a buy-and-sell list for the portfolio, these trades remain to be executed. Equity market-neutral managers devise systems to ensure that their traders execute the trades correctly and at the lowest possible cost. Three main costs must be considered in the trading process:

1. *Opportunity costs.* The cost of not getting their best ideas into the portfolio in a timely fashion.
2. *Market impact.* The impact that implementing a position can have on the market price of that particular stock.
3. *Commissions.* The cost of the trade.

Manager Styles—Putting It All Together

An equity market-neutral or statistical arbitrage manager's style is dictated by how the manager puts the different components of his or her equity market-neutral strategy together. The strategy involves not only the factors the manager chooses for the model, but how many factors (some managers believe that more factors are better; others warn against dilution of predictive value or "overfitting"), how those factors work together, which risk factors are neutralized, and so forth. In the end, an equity market-neutral strategy becomes a balancing act. Equity market-neutral managers must harness the power of quantitative models without erasing any advantage through their overuse. Managers must periodically question how well the model creates an optimal bundle of risk and reward.

In addition to methods of initial screens, stock selection, and portfolio construction, a number of other points can differentiate one manager from the next.

The method and frequency with which managers rebalance their portfolios can distinguish equity market-neutral managers from each other. As discussed earlier, buy and sell rules are usually based on the relative rankings produced by the multifactor model of expected returns. How a manager chooses to set up his or her rules (e.g., whether the manager sells long positions that slip into the second decile, or waits until they fall into the third decile) determines how much trading the manager does, how much turnover the portfolio experiences, and what the transaction costs will be.

These rules also reflect the time horizon for positions. Managers who are looking to exploit short-term price moves reflect this strategy in the factors they use as well as in a higher rate of turnover compared to a manager with a longer-term outlook.

Transaction costs and impact on market price are often part of the optimization process. Trade opportunities can be forgone when the cost of completing the transaction is not merited by its potential benefits. Buy and sell rules usually work within the framework of risk–return optimization. Exceptions include stocks that are involved in announced mergers or in other corporate events.

Another key point of differentiation among equity market-neutral managers and more quantitatively oriented statistical arbitrageurs is the level of human discretion they allow in their investment process. For example, what level of qualitative analysis does the manager perform in addition to the analysis of the quantitative model. Common qualitative factors involving manager discretion include reviewing buy-and-sell lists to identify anomalies that the quantitative model would not pick up, such as pending involvement in mergers or acquisitions, late breaking news, stocks subject to excessive rumors, or faulty data.

Because markets are always changing and stock prices are driven by different forces, some factors that had predictive power in the past may lose their predictive power in the future. Equity market-neutral managers and statistical arbitrageurs must determine when and if to drop factors from their models and/or to add new ones. If the goal is to create a model that will approximate investor behavior, then keeping a model dynamic requires a certain level of vigilance. Deciding which factors to use and how to weight them is an important part of any equity market-neutral or statistical arbitrage strategy.

SOURCE OF RETURN

Equity market-neutral managers derive returns from the performance of their long portfolio *relative* their short portfolio; in other words, from their long–short spread. This *relationship between stocks* may not necessarily be less volatile than the stock market as a whole, although it has seemed to be so over the past few years. It is important to note that although equity market-neutral managers invest in equities, their source of return is entirely different from that of a traditional long-only manager. The risk to an equity market-neutral strategy is *relative* stock-picking risk rather than *absolute* stock-picking risk. The strategy does not require all long positions to go up and all short positions to go down. It is only necessary for the long positions to outperform the short positions. Equity market-neutral managers feel that, with the aid of powerful quantitative models, they can manage this relationship between securities better than they can predict the fate of any particular stock or of the market as a whole.

Many managers describe equity market neutral as unemotional. The models that determine the portfolios make it possible for managers to make decisions devoid of personal problems and an occasional bad day. Equity market-neutral managers believe that, in the long run, a system based on factors that have proven to have predictive value is more disciplined than a system that involves human emotion and intuition. These managers go to great lengths to eliminate systemic market risks and isolate their quantitative models. By doing so, they take on model risk—the risk that their quantitative system is flawed or does not have the predictive power it was thought to have.

The stock market is dynamic. Quantitative models and the managers who create them require time to react to changes in the market. These two facts periodically create situations in which static factors in quantitative models must be reconsidered in light of rapid and dynamic changes in the factors driving stock prices. Managers must ask model-specific questions, such as whether the model's traditional value factors will have any predictive power for Internet stocks.

RECENT GROWTH AND DEVELOPMENTS IN EQUITY MARKET-NEUTRAL INVESTING

Equity market-neutral and statistical arbitrage have grown from 2 percent of hedge fund assets in 1990 to over 10 percent in 1999.

This dramatic increase has been fueled by record growth in equity markets, consistent risk-adjusted performance, and investors' preference for the downside protection offered by a fully hedged equity portfolio. In addition, improved quantitative models and technological innovations have reduced infrastructure costs and made equity market-neutral strategies an option for smaller money managers.

Although few equity market-neutral managers kept pace with upside equity markets in 1998, the strategy showed its ability to provide downside protection during the month of August. While the S&P 500 dropped over 14.5 percent and the Russell 2000 Small-Cap Index was down over 19 percent, the HFRI Equity Market-Neutral Index returned –1.67 percent. Nevertheless, the momentum-driven environment confounded many models based on value factors and tested the model conviction of all managers in the sector.

Beginning in May 1998, a flight to growth stocks occurred in the U.S. equity market. The utter rejection of value stocks by investors, in favor of price momentum, produced the widest disparity between the two investing styles since detailed data began to be collected in 1970. One manager estimated that, for his universe of stocks, the spread between long and short selections, based solely on traditional measures of growth and momentum, was a positive 30 percent in 1998 (the long side outperformed the short side by 30 percent). In contrast, the same manager estimated that the spread between long and short selections, based solely on traditional measures of value, was a negative 38 percent in 1998 (the long side underperformed the short side by 38 percent).

A similar disconnection between large-cap stocks and small-cap stocks occurred during the second half of 1998. In August 1998, after posting its largest single-month loss for the 1990s, the S&P 500 Index recovered to post 28.55 percent returns for the year. But it is important to note that the S&P 500 Index is capitalization weighted; therefore, gains made by large-cap issues masked poorer performance by the broader equity markets. The components that make up a style, such as growth or value, are predictive stock selection factors, whereas capitalization is generally thought of as a risk factor. Therefore, what can be considered "normal" historical relationships and correlations among stocks, groups of stocks, predictive factors, and risk factors did not necessarily hold during this period. Because many market-neutral managers used optimizers that were based on such correlations, it is questionable whether the optimization process added any value.

As shown in Figure 9.4, the stock market bottomed out in the first week of October as concerns about liquidity and global financial stability peaked. Subsequently, the Japanese pushed through a banking bill, and the Federal Reserve cut interest rates for a second time in a three-week span, restoring liquidity and confidence to the U.S. market. Led by large-capitalization issues, technology stocks, and financial stocks, U.S. stocks staged a rally during which they

Figure 9.4 Selected U.S. Stock Indexes, July 1, 1998 to December 31, 1998

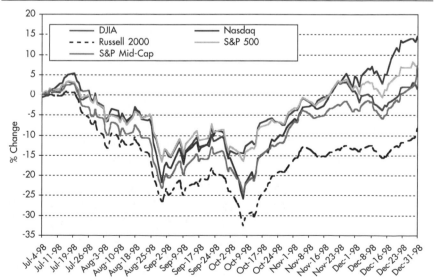

recovered most of what they had lost, and in some cases pushed into positive territory. By comparison, the HFRI Equity Market-Neutral Index showed returns of –0.61 percent in October, 0.85 percent in November, and 3.59 percent in December, and the HFRI Statistical Arbitrage Index returned 0.46 percent, 1.38 percent, and 2.24 percent, compared with 8.13 percent, 6.06 percent, and 5.76 percent in the same periods for the S&P 500.

The more significant issue for equity market-neutral managers during the period was the way certain factors (in particular, P/E ratios, P/B ratios, and other traditional measures of value) did not exhibit the same predictive value as they have historically. To some extent, investors' emphasis on growth investing, at the expense of value investing, is part of a natural style rotation. Investors who have reaped huge gains from increasing share prices (as an increasing number of U.S. investors did in the 1990s' bull market) tend to focus on the future and earnings potential. However, when the momentum slows or even reverses, that emphasis

Table 9.1   HFRI Equity Market-Neutral Returns, 1990–1999

Number of Funds	Average Size (Millions of $US)	Year	Jan	Feb	Mar	Apr	May
8	14	1990	1.23	1.23	0.82	0.73	0.50
10	19	1991	2.51	0.04	2.70	–0.01	–0.02
15	22	1992	0.36	0.96	0.58	–0.03	0.11
19	22	1993	1.91	1.06	1.67	–0.14	0.58
25	89	1994	0.78	0.58	0.44	0.92	–0.95
31	75	1995	0.22	1.42	1.77	1.86	0.60
34	70	1996	2.18	0.95	0.86	0.35	1.39
38	133	1997	1.20	0.12	0.43	0.96	1.49
78	136	1998	0.54	0.76	1.26	0.66	0.48
48	185	1999	0.15	–1.33	–0.76	–0.65	0.17

* Annual represents geometric compounded average.

tends to shift to the present and current earnings. It remains to be seen whether the new generation of retail investors and the explosion of financial technology and available data have changed this relationship in a permanent way.

Equity market-neutral managers were also affected by larger macro-financial events. Russia's default on its internal debt set off a flight to quality in which investors pulled money out of stocks in favor of the safety of Treasury bonds. Thus, equity market-neutral managers who had long positions in stocks because of those stocks' fundamental factors saw their long portfolios lose value—not because of any change in the underlying fundamentals of the companies, but because the long-only community was pulling money out of all equities. In addition, equity market-neutral managers were affected by events particular to managers' employing the strategy, or cross-arbitrage players' carrying equity market-neutral portfolios. Managers who shared factors with other players who were forced to liquidate positions for nonfundamental reasons

Jun	Jul	Aug	Sep	Oct	Nov	Dec	Annual*
1.37	0.77	1.80	1.81	1.37	0.83	2.01	15.45
0.56	2.50	0.28	1.92	0.97	1.17	2.07	15.65
0.62	1.24	−0.35	1.17	1.04	1.18	1.54	8.73
2.37	0.63	0.91	2.44	−0.10	−1.45	0.77	11.11
0.58	0.37	−0.35	0.02	−0.12	−0.45	0.82	2.65
0.92	2.23	0.98	1.85	1.58	0.78	1.03	16.33
1.37	1.62	0.78	0.66	2.10	0.16	0.95	14.20
1.54	2.17	0.21	2.18	1.36	0.53	0.67	13.66
1.69	−0.27	−1.67	0.81	−0.61	0.85	3.59	8.30
2.02	1.91	0.70	0.89	1.00	1.10	5.26	10.80

Table 9.2   HFRI Statistical Arbitrage Returns, 1990–1999

Number of Funds	Average Size (Millions of $US)	Year	Jan	Feb	Mar	Apr	May
6	10	1990	0.83	1.02	0.48	−0.18	1.72
9	15	1991	4.46	1.81	1.21	1.06	1.79
15	19	1992	0.16	1.84	1.68	0.85	−0.07
18	38	1993	2.24	1.47	1.97	−0.38	0.62
19	191	1994	1.52	−0.19	−0.40	1.08	−0.70
23	139	1995	0.33	1.99	1.16	1.59	1.58
25	115	1996	2.42	1.32	1.30	−0.08	1.11
32	144	1997	1.04	0.91	0.49	2.23	1.21
42	147	1998	−0.05	1.47	1.85	0.52	1.11
29	99	1999	−0.98	−1.14	−2.00	−0.23	0.49

* Annual represents geometric compounded average.

experienced negative performance. It was not necessary for the managers to hold the exact same position to get hurt, because a sell-off in one stock could have prompted sell-offs in similar, correlated stocks.

Equity market-neutral and statistical arbitrage managers had a difficult year in 1999. Anecdotal evidence suggests that some managers have since adjusted their models to reflect the emphasis on momentum investing (as evidenced by the rebound in the second half of the less quantitatively oriented Equity Market-Neutral Index). On the other hand, stock market valuations have continued to defy traditional valuation rules, which has resulted in poor performance for statistical arbitrageurs. A return to more rational valuations in the future would benefit these strategies. Tables 9.1 on pages 226–227 and 9.2 show the returns for the HFRI Equity Market-Neutral and the HFRI Statistical Arbitrage indices. Figures 9.5 and 9.6 show the growth of $1,000 invested in each of the strategies

Jun	Jul	Aug	Sep	Oct	Nov	Dec	Annual*
1.61	0.98	−0.31	−0.33	0.81	2.18	1.88	11.19
−0.50	2.39	0.44	1.01	0.30	−0.19	2.85	17.84
0.51	1.53	−0.38	0.55	−0.17	0.96	2.86	10.77
2.85	0.86	1.15	2.08	−0.89	−0.98	1.04	12.62
0.21	0.87	0.86	−0.75	0.55	−0.03	1.59	4.67
1.08	2.01	0.59	1.80	0.87	0.63	−0.21	14.25
1.96	1.20	0.45	1.42	3.44	2.28	1.28	19.63
2.16	3.60	−0.25	2.21	1.31	1.44	1.53	19.36
1.90	−0.39	−1.03	0.15	0.60	1.38	2.24	10.14
1.98	1 23	0.02	0.12	0.46	−0.45	−0.76	−1.32

Figure 9.5 Equity Market Neutral: Growth of $1,000, January 1990–December 1999

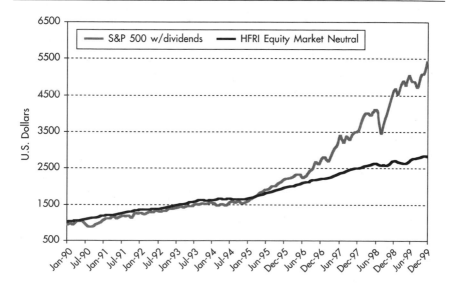

Figure 9.6 Statistical Arbitrage: Growth of $1,000, January 1990–December 1999

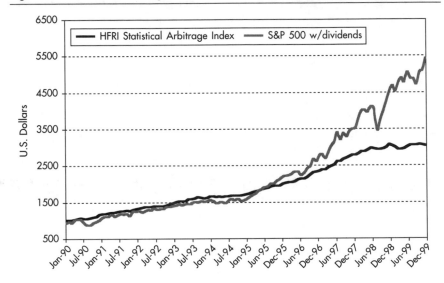

in 1990. Note that Statistical Arbitrage was disaggregated from Equity Market Neutral in 1999, to more accurately reflect the highly quantitative nature of this sub-strategy. The Statistical Arbitrage Index returns for 1990 to 1998 were calculated based on the historical returns for the managers in the index.

Relative Value Arbitrage *10*

Relative value arbitrage managers are usually practitioners of multiple investment strategies. Their overall emphasis is on making "spread trades," which derive returns from the relationship between two related securities rather than from the direction of the market. Generally, relative value arbitrageurs take offsetting long and short positions in similar or related securities when their values, which are mathematically or historically interrelated, are temporarily distorted. They realize a profit when the skewed relationship between the securities returns to normal.

Rather than trying to guess the direction in which the market will go, managers neutralize their overall position by taking both long and short positions. Relative value managers add value by determining which relative value strategies offer the best opportunities at any given time, and weighting that strategy accordingly in their overall portfolio. Relative value strategies may include forms of fixed-income arbitrage, including mortgage-backed arbitrage, merger arbitrage, convertible arbitrage, statistical arbitrage, pairs trading, options and warrants trading, capital structure arbitrage, and structured discount convertibles (more commonly known as Regulation D securities) arbitrage.

RELATIVE VALUE ARBITRAGE APPROACHES

Relative value arbitrage, by definition, involves more than one investment strategy. A manager who engages in only a single strategy is properly classified as a practitioner of that strategy. Traditionally, relative value managers have been described as one of two types. The first type engages in two or more closely related strategies, such as convertible arbitrage and warrants, or warrants and options, or convertible arbitrage and Regulation D securities. The securities involved in these strategies have either shared features (e.g., the use of option pricing models in their analysis) or structural similarities. The second type of manager engages in strategies that are less closely related, such as merger arbitrage and convertible arbitrage, or fixed-income arbitrage and pairs trading. These managers generally split their operation into different units for each strategy. As a result, asset allocation is paramount. The manager may risk overextending assets into strategies in which he or she has little expertise, simply to increase returns.

Relative value managers, therefore, can be distinguished from one another by the strategies they use. The possible strategies span a continuum from harder arbitrage plays, such as convertible arbitrage and merger arbitrage, which have structural features by which managers may force price convergence, to more theoretical arbitrages such as the more subjective fixed-income arbitrage trades, which provide no way to force a convergence of the prices of the two securities. The strategies that relative value managers are apt to use are described briefly here, and cross-references are given for strategies that are covered in depth in previous chapters.

Convertible Arbitrage

A convertible arbitrage trade is a relative value play on the relationship between a convertible security and its underlying stock. Generally, the strategy involves constructing long portfolios of convertible bonds and hedging these positions by selling short the underlying stock of each bond. Convertible bonds—bonds that can be converted into a fixed number of shares of the issuing company's stock—are hybrid securities that have features of a bond and of stock; therefore, their valuations reflect both types of instruments. Usually, the price of the convertible declines less rapidly than the underlying stock in a falling equity market, and mirrors the price of the stock more closely in a rising equity market. Convertible arbitrage strategies try to extract profits from these complex pricing relationships by purchasing the convertible bond and selling short its underlying stock in an amount that neutralizes the effect of stock price movements on the price of the convertible.

At least six separate components are embedded in the market price of a convertible security. A convertible bond responds to different market forces, not just to its underlying common stock. In fact, the price of a convertible bond almost never corresponds exactly to the price of its underlying common stock. For example, the price of a convertible bond tends to move inversely to changes in interest rates because of its bond characteristics, but the price of its underlying common stock reacts to the perceived macroeconomic causes and effects of such interest-rate fluctuations.

There is no single formula for calculating the movement of a convertible security as a function of the price of its underlying equity, but several factors have varying levels of predictive value. Convertible bond specialists make arbitrage profits by identifying pricing disparities between convertible bonds and their underlying equity, and then tightly monitoring the factors that can change these relationships.

For a detailed description of convertible arbitrage strategies, see Chapter 4.

Merger Arbitrage

Merger arbitrage trades are relative value plays on the relationship of the stock prices of two companies involved in an announced merger. Generally, the strategy involves buying the common stock of a company that is being acquired, or merging with another company and selling short the stock of the acquiring company. The target company's stock typically trades at a discount to the value that it will attain after the merger is completed. This occurs for two reasons:

1. Corporate acquisitions are generally made at a premium to the stock price of the target company prior to the announcement of the proposed merger.
2. All mergers involve event risk—that is, risk that the transaction will fail to be completed as announced.

If a transaction fails to be completed, then the price of the target company's stock usually declines—sometimes, dramatically. Merger arbitrage strategies make profits when they correctly anticipate the outcome of an announced merger and capture the spread between the current market price of the target company's stock and the price it appreciates to when the deal is completed.

A disparity between the price of the acquiring company's stock and the price of the target company's stock is called a *merger arbitrage spread*. Two key factors determine its size. The first factor is the size of the premium over the target company's stock price that the acquirer is willing to pay. Although many variables can affect how large a premium an acquiring firm is willing to pay, a premium is almost always offered (and most target companies would not accept less than their present market value, as represented by their market capitalization).

The second factor contributing to the size of the merger arbitrage spread is the uncertainty about whether the deal will be completed. Until the deal is consummated, the prices of both stocks usually reflect the market's uncertainty, which can be generated by any number of factors, including, but not confined to, financing difficulties, regulatory roadblocks, complicated deal structures, management issues, market sentiment, and the emergence of new negative information about one of the firms. Often, because of this uncertainty, the target company's stock trades at a discount to the value it will attain if the deal is completed.

Merger arbitrage specialists usually (1) translate an arbitrage spread into an annualized rate of return, (2) estimate the probability that the deal will go through, and (3) determine whether the returns to be derived from the spread (if the deal is completed) offer sufficient compensation for the estimated risk of the deal's failing. As a general rule, friendly deals involving large-capitalization companies produce tighter spreads and moderate rates of return; more complex deals, and those involving small-capitalization firms, usually produce wider spreads and higher rates of return.

Merger arbitrage specialists do not try to anticipate possible merger activity. If they did, they would be investing on the basis of rumors. Instead, they research announced mergers and acquisitions and reduce their uncertainty about each of the possible outcomes. Before taking a position, they review public corporate documents of the firms, historical financial statements for each of the firms, EDGAR Fed filings, analysts' reports, standard media releases, conference calls, and conversations with the companies' managers and industry contacts. When they feel that the rate of return implicit in the spread is significantly more than the actual risk of the deal's failing to be completed, they invest in the merger. Generally, they add to positions as more positive information becomes available, as market sentiment toward the deal solidifies, and as the outcome of the transaction becomes more certain. Alternatively, a merger arbitrage manager liquidates an investment position when new negative information is uncovered and the potential return no longer sufficiently outweighs the perceived risks of holding the position. If all goes as planned, the position is not liquidated until the transaction is consummated.

For a detailed description of merger arbitrage strategies, see Chapter 7.

Equity Statistical Arbitrage

Equity statistical arbitrage involves creating groups of stocks that are fundamentally similar in some aspect, and then trying to exploit anomalous, purely statistical relationships between stocks within each group. Most common among these relationships is the tendency of the valuations of similar stocks to revert to the mean of the group. Stocks with valuations above the mean of the group are sold short, and stocks with valuations below the mean are held long. (The expectation is that both sides will eventually converge on the mean of the group.) The similarity to equity market-neutral investing is apparent in that stocks expected to outperform the market are held long, and stocks expected to underperform the market are sold short in equal dollar amounts. In essence, statistical arbitrage builds portfolios of spread trades within carefully defined groups.

For a detailed description of equity statistical arbitrage strategies, see Chapter 9.

Pairs Trading

Explicit pairs trading is an example of a highly qualitative form of equity market-neutral investing. It involves going long on a stock in a specific sector or industry, and pairing that trade specifically with an equal dollar-value short position in a stock in the same industry or sector. Philosophically, the strategy tries to insulate the portfolio from systemic moves in sectors or industries by being long in the best stock in the industry and shorting the worst. Profit is derived from the difference in price change between the two stocks, rather than from the direction in which each stock moves. Thus, the strategy does not require that the long position go up and the short position go down; a profit can be earned if the long goes up more than the short or the short goes down more than the long.

Fixed-Income Arbitrage

Fixed-income arbitrage strategies involve investing in one or more fixed-income securities and hedging against underlying market risk by simultaneously investing in another fixed-income security. These trades seek to capture profit opportunities presented by usually small pricing anomalies while maintaining minimum exposure to interest rates and other systemic market risks. In most cases, fixed-income arbitrageurs take offsetting long and short positions in similar fixed-income securities that are mathematically or historically interrelated, when that relationship is temporarily distorted by market events, investor preferences, exogenous shocks to supply or demand, or structural features of the fixed-income market. These positions could include corporate debt, Treasury securities, U.S. agency debt, sovereign debt, municipal debt, or the sovereign debt of emerging market countries. Often, trades involve swaps and futures.

By purchasing cheap fixed-income securities and selling short an equal amount of expensive fixed-income securities, fixed-income arbitrageurs protect themselves from changes in interest rates that systematically affect the prices of all fixed-income securities. If they select instruments that respond to interest-rate changes similarly, then an interest rate rise that adversely affects the long position will have an offsetting positive effect on the short position. In fixed-income terminology, they do not make directional duration bets. They realize a profit when the skewed relationship between the securities returns to a normal range. Rather than trying to guess the direction in which the market will go, they neutralize interest rate changes and derive profit from their ability to identify similar securities that are mispriced relative to one another. Because the prices of fixed-income instruments are based on yield curves, volatility curves, expected cash flows, credit ratings, and special bond and option features, they must use sophisticated analytical models to identify true pricing disparities. The complexity of fixed-income pricing is actually essential to fixed-income arbitrageurs. They rely on market events, investors with different incentives and constraints, investors with different modes of analysis, and investors who are less sophisticated than themselves to create relatively over- and undervalued fixed-income securities and, thus, profit opportunities.

For a detailed description of fixed-income arbitrage strategies, see Chapter 5.

Options and Warrants Trading

Options and warrants strategies involve relative value plays on the relationship between a stock's price and a stock option. Often, these trades are constructed so that there is no implicit directional bet on the price of the stock. Instead, the bet concerns the volatility (or magnitude) of stock price movements, up or down.

A typical options trade, constructed to extract value from stock price volatility by using options, would look something like this:

- Stock price at $50.
- Buy 2 call contracts, 6 months out and with a strike price of 50, for $5 a share (2 × 5 × 100 shares = $1,000).
- Sell short 100 shares at $50 ($1,000 × 50 = $5,000).

The trade creates a position with both a definable downside and a potential upside if volatility increases, regardless of direction. The worst-case scenario for the trade would be to lose the $1,000 on the options contracts. But if the stock price exceeds a certain price range, on either the upside or the downside, the position will be profitable. This trade would be referred to as "buying volatility." Depending on the circumstances, managers may buy or sell volatility in index products or particular stocks. They may even play the index volatility against that of particular stocks. In any case, managers are always trying to create a cheap option and limit downside risk.

A second example of an options-based strategy is a split-strike conversion strategy. The strategy involves buying a basket of macro-capitalization stocks and hedging them with Options Exchange Index (OEX) options. The hedge is achieved by selling out-of-the-money OEX call options and purchasing OEX put options at or out of the money to match the size of the underlying portfolio. (A call option is out of the money when its strike price is higher than the current price of the underlying index. A put option is out of the money when its strike price is below the price of the underlying index.) The sale of OEX calls against the basket of stocks increases the standstill rate of return, while also allowing for additional returns if the stock portfolio goes up to the strike price. The put options protect the underlying equity portfolio from downward movement and are usually funded with the proceeds of the sale of the calls and any dividends paid out by the underlying basket of equities.

Capital Structure Arbitrage

Capital structure arbitrage involves buying one level of a company's capital structure and shorting another. Examples of different levels are voting vs. nonvoting shares, the stock of a holding company vs. the stock of a subsidiary, or cross ownership plays known as stub trades.

An example of a stub trade is as follows. A manager buys stock in an insurance company that owns a number of other companies in other businesses (which issue stock separately) and simultaneously hedges out the insurance company's ownership interest in the other companies so that he or she owns purely the insurance company. The stock of the insurance company is trading at half book value, but when its ownership of other businesses is hedged out, the isolated insurance company is worth 2 × book value, and the stock pays a $2.60 dividend. The spread between the stock price of the whole company and the stock prices of the related companies sold short is $5.00. Essentially, then, the manager has created an instrument that costs $5.00 and pays a dividend of $2.60. This state of affairs won't last long, so the manager sells out of the position when the spread widens, making the dividend more expensive.

Regulation D (Structured Discount Convertible) Arbitrage

Most practitioners of Regulation D strategies refer to the deals involving this instrument as "structured discount convertibles," or a similar term. The securities issued under the auspices of Regulation D are privately offered to investment managers by companies in need of timely financing.

An example would be convertible subordinated debentures (three-year maturity) with three-year warrants, an interest rate of 5 percent, and negotiated provisions to convert each debenture into the issuing company's common stock. The terms of any particular deal reflect the negotiating strength of the issuing company. With smaller companies that have more risk, managers are often able to negotiate an explicit discount. Large-capitalization companies often do not give an explicit discount; instead, they make the conversion price dependent on a look-back period (e.g., the average of the two lowest trading prices over the past 21 days). Managers often negotiate a price-reset feature for a security, to limit downside risk.

After a deal is closed, there is a waiting period while the private share offering is registered with the SEC. The managers can convert these instruments into only private shares, and they cannot trade the convertibles publicly during the waiting period; therefore, their investment is illiquid until it becomes registered. As a result, the securities must be priced subjectively, at the manager's discretion. Most managers hedge the position with common stock until the registration becomes effective, and then liquidate the position gradually over 60 to 180 days.

Risks and Risk Control

Relative value arbitrage strategies have three primary risks: (1) strategy-specific risks, (2) the risk of the chosen strategy mix, and (3) the risk of the strategy weightings. The strategy-specific risks of convertible arbitrage, fixed-income arbitrage, mortgage-backed securities arbitrage, merger arbitrage, and statistical arbitrage are described in earlier chapters. It is beyond the scope of this book to discuss all of the specifics for other, less prevalent strategies mentioned in this chapter. However, it is important to note that all of them involve the risk that the spread between the long and the short component will widen because of unanticipated market events.

Strategy Mix

A defining characteristic of any relative value manager is the particular mix of strategies he or she has available. The number of strategies included in a portfolio is usually a function of resources and expertise. Potential gains from adding another strategy to the mix can be erased by inexperience and insufficient comprehension of the strategy. A manager must balance the freedom to move between strategies with the potential gains from specialization. Certain strategies have obvious crossovers and synergies, such as Regulation D and convertible arbitrage, or convertibles and options, or statistical arbitrage and pairs trading.

Strategy Weightings

In addition to the skill they exhibit within the relative value strategies they use, relative value managers must be adept at recognizing the strategies that offer the best return and risk characteristics at any given time. To make prudent decisions about strategy weightings, managers need to have a macro view of how the different components of the financial world interact and affect one another.

Source of Return

Relative value arbitrage has a nondirectional philosophical orientation that qualifies it to be included in discussions of market-neutral strategies. In other words, the strategies utilized by relative value arbitrage managers are based on the relationship between two or more securities rather than on market direction. These strategies construct trades involving related securities for which the historical price relationship is temporarily out of sync. Some managers construct a "synthetic option" that allows them to buy the potential upside at a limited and defined cost that represents the worst-case scenario. In normal market environments, relative value strategies show very little correlation to general market indexes, indicating that returns are derived from other sources. Nevertheless, as with many investment strategies, these alternative sources of return can become vulnerable in serious and unexpected market downturns. Thus, the relationship between securities, although not necessarily a more stable source of return than the market, is certainly a different and nondirectional one. As multiple-strategy managers, relative value arbitrageurs derive returns from their ability to allocate capital to the best opportunities. However, they are always at risk of spreading themselves too thin or venturing into markets that are outside their expertise.

Growth and Recent Developments in Relative Value Arbitrage

Relative value arbitrage, as a strategy, decreased from 10 percent of hedge fund assets in 1990 to just over 2 percent in 1999. This decline does not reflect reduced assets in the strategy, or poor performance, so much as it indicates rapid growth in other strategies and increased specialization among managers, which has led to some reclassifications of managers to more specific strategies.

Some of the potential risks to relative value arbitrage were exposed during the second half of 1998. The managers included in the HFRI Relative Value Index showed an average return of 2.81 percent for the year, and a negative return for the second half, including −5.80 percent in August. These figures may understate actual losses during the period. They do not include losses sustained by Long Term Capital Management (LTCM), which was involved in much more relative value arbitrage than most market observers had suspected. Strategywise, the biggest losers were fixed-income arbitrageurs and managers whose trades matched a long position in a less liquid security against a short position in a more liquid security.

Contributing to the problem was an overextension by certain managers (LTCM being foremost among them) of leveraged capital into multiple strategies with the intention of increasing returns. LTCM's extension into merger arbitrage was a good example. LTCM was said to have had a 4-million-share position in Ciena–Tellabs, a high-profile merger deal that was called off in

Table 10.1   Relative Value Arbitrage Returns, 1990–1999

Number of Funds	Average Size (Millions of $US)	Year	Jan	Feb	Mar	Apr	May
5	84	1990	0.84	1.67	1.90	1.50	1.57
7	39	1991	2.59	3.10	2.66	1.80	0.70
10	37	1992	5.72	2.60	−0.79	2.12	1.95
13	39	1993	2.33	0.90	3.68	2.40	2.46
19	35	1994	2.48	0.44	0.33	−0.42	−0.14
29	34	1995	1.28	1.09	0.63	1.57	0.76
32	61	1996	1.46	1.43	1.15	2.04	1.74
30	87	1997	1.38	1.09	−0.66	1.30	1.83
41	166	1998	1.98	1.39	1.57	1.93	0.30
38	132	1999	2.61	0.11	0.57	2.80	1.17

* Annual represents geometric compounded average.

early September, at a high level of leverage. (See Chapter 7.) LTCM was forced to liquidate its position at the worst possible time, to support the less liquid positions on its books. The overriding factor across all strategies became liquidity during the period, and events in one strategy created ripples in other unrelated strategies. Relative value arbitrage managers found that previously uncorrelated strategies in their portfolio became correlated.

Those managers who were not forced to reduce leverage and sell positions at depressed prices took mark-to-market losses but recovered much of their losses in the months that followed. A small number of managers were in a position to buy fundamentally sound positions at depressed prices. Managers who constrained themselves to strategies in which they had a high level of expertise were generally better off than those who were spread too thin. In any case, the period made quite obvious the importance of and the risks associated with asset allocation for relative value arbitrage managers.

Jun	Jul	Aug	Sep	Oct	Nov	Dec	Annual*
0.96	1.35	−0.46	1.04	0.56	1.32	0.40	13.38
−0.45	1.44	0.51	2.03	−0.51	0.66	−1.19	14.07
2.46	2.05	0.61	0.33	0.51	1.74	1.11	22.26
1.63	1.76	2.11	1.34	1.81	1.09	2.74	27.10
0.22	1.08	0.14	−0.28	0.13	0.04	−0.06	4.00
1.72	1.18	1.34	1.40	0.36	1.68	1.64	15.66
0.99	−0.58	1.53	0.80	0.17	1.02	1.89	14.49
1.93	1.57	1.43	1.86	0.96	1.31	0.90	16.10
0.16	−0.51	−5.80	0.19	−0.48	1.66	0.63	2.81
1.37	0.83	0.80	0.49	0.59	1.28	2.00	15.60

Figure 10.1   Relative Value Arbitrage: Growth of $1,000, January 1990–December 1999

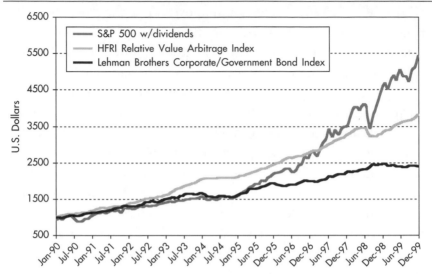

Relative value strategies showed great resilience in 1999; all of the primary underlying strategies exhibited returns in line with, or above, their historical averages. Ample liquidity in the U.S. markets, and recovering economies in Europe and Asia, provided a good atmosphere for relative value trades. Table 10.1 on the preceding pages and Figure 10.1 above illustrate the historical returns for the strategy.

Afterword

A friend once told me a story about a dog that walked himself. A large German shepherd, this dog lived across from the city park. To get to the park, the dog had to cross a very busy street.

To cross the street, the dog found a solution. Each day he would position himself prominently on the corner, face the on-coming traffic, and aggressively bark at the cars driving by. Eventually, they would stop, and the dog, very much in control of his world, would confidently proceed across the street. On his return home, he would repeat his barking procedure and cross the street when the traffic stopped.

But one day on his return home from the park, the cars would not stop for him no matter how loud he barked. The dog became bewildered, no longer in control of his world. The reality of the situation was that the traffic stopping had nothing to do with the dog's barking and everything to do with the traffic light on the corner. A decision by the city regarding traffic flow had resulted in the removal of the traffic light, leaving the dog stranded.

Analyzing hedge-fund strategies and making investment decisions involves a high degree of reliance on understanding true cause-and-effect relationships. As I work on such endeavors, I keep this story in mind and try to avoid making the same mistake that the dog made in confusing cause and effect. To do so I need to do more than identify what appears to be cause-and-effect relation-ships; I need to identify whether there is actually a nexus between the two.

One of the most serious flaws in evaluating market-neutral strategies and managers is overreliance on past activities and performance, good or bad, as an indicator of suitability to the investor's needs. That a manager or investment approach has generated certain levels of return, or that those returns have certain statistical relationships with those of other asset classes, is not enough to base expectations of future performance. If the evaluation process does not identify and consider the underlying and perhaps less evident factors driving returns, its usefulness is no different than barking at cars, as there is no nexus between the action and the observed result.

A successful investor in this field must be careful not to be fooled by appearances. The reality of these market-neutral investment strategies can only be understood by looking beneath the surface. I hope this book has helped to provide the concepts and tools to accomplish the task.

Glossary

Asset swap.   An exchange of cash flows between two parties.

Basis trades.   The purchase of a government bond and the simultaneous sale of futures contracts on that bond.

Bearish hedge.   Sometimes known as a short-biased hedge. Occurs when a convertible arbitrageur sells short more shares than are required to maintain neutrality for movements in the price of the underlying stock.

Bullish hedge.   Sometimes known as a long-biased hedge. Occurs when a convertible arbitrageur sells short fewer shares than are required to maintain neutrality for movements in the price of the underlying stock.

Busted convertibles.   Convertible bonds trading well below par value, at or near their investment value.

Call feature.   A feature that allows the issuer to redeem a bond before it matures.

Cash merger.   A deal in which the acquiring company pays cash for the target company.

Catalyst.   A near-term event, such as a press release or a new-product launch, that will heighten investor interest in, or change the market's perception of, a company.

Collar.   A range of stock prices, outside of which a merger target will receive additional shares in a stock swap merger, or, in an extreme case, can call off a potential merger.

Collateral.   Cash or very liquid securities that are held as a deposit on borrowed securities.

Collateralized mortgage obligations (CMOs).   Structures created by pooling pools of mortgage collateral and issuing specialized securities based on the resulting pool.

Conversion premium.   The amount an investor pays for a convertible bond in excess of the amount that the investor would have received if he or she had converted it into the underlying common stock. In essence, it represents the value of the option to convert the bond to stock. The relevant equation is:

$$\text{Conversion premium} = \frac{(\text{Price of convertible} - \text{Conversion value})}{\text{Conversion value}}.$$

249

Conversion price. The effective price for conversion into stock with the convertible bond at par.

Conversion ratio. The number of shares of common stock a convertible bondholder would receive per bond, upon converting the bond to the underlying stock. The relevant equation is:

$$\text{Conversion ratio} = \frac{\text{Par value}}{\text{Conversion price}}.$$

Conversion value. The value of the equity side of the convertible—the value of the bond, at any given time, if it were converted to the underlying common stock at the current market price. The relevant equation is:

$$\text{Conversion value} = \text{Conversion ratio} \times \text{Price of common stock}.$$

Convertible bonds. Bonds that can be converted into a fixed number of shares of the issuing company's stock.

Convexity. A measure of the degree to which a bond's duration changes as its yield to maturity changes.

Correlation. A term from regression analysis that describes the strength of the relationship between a dependent and an independent variable. Assets, or strategies, are correlated if the returns they provide are similar to one another in similar market environments.

Counterparty. A relationship between financial entities, either as a borrower of securities or a lender.

Delta. A number that reflects how the price of a convertible security will respond to a movement in the price of the underlying stock. It is calculated by taking the slope of the tangent line to the convertible price curve at the current price.

Derivatives. Any financial instrument for which the value is directly dependent on the price of another asset. Good examples include options (the price of a stock option depends on the price of the underlying stock) and futures contracts (the price of a futures contract depends on the price of the underlying asset).

Directional exposure. The amount of risk an *unhedged* position faces in the market as compared to the net exposure of positions involving long and short hedged relationships.

Duration. A measure of how sensitive a bond's price is to a shift in interest rates. Roughly:

$$\text{Duration} = \frac{\text{Change in price} / \text{Price}}{\text{Change in interest rates}}.$$

Event analysis. A process by which an analyst assesses the probabilities of all the possible outcomes of a corporate event.

Exposure. The amount of risk a position faces in the market. Because particular markets contain risks, taking a position in one of these markets "exposes" the investor to that market's risks. For example, investors might have exposure not only to equities, fixed income, or currency, but also to sub-sets, such as market sectors.

Fundamental value. The intrinsic or "real" value of a security, reflecting both tangible and intangible company assets.

Growth stocks. Stocks that an investor believes will appreciate because the companies' output and earnings will grow in the future.

Hedging. Any investment that is taken in conjunction with another position in order to reduce directional exposure. A classic example is farmers who enter into futures contracts for grain, to lock in a particular price. They remove any uncertainty about the price they will receive for the grain, but they forgo the possibility of receiving a higher price.

Investment premium. The difference between the market value of a convertible bond and its investment value, expressed as a percentage of the investment value. The relevant equation is:

$$\text{Investment premium} = \frac{(\text{Market price} - \text{Investment value})}{\text{Investment value}}.$$

Investment value. The value of the bond component of a convertible bond, which serves as a kind of investment floor for the security.

Leverage. The use of borrowed funds or of derivatives to create exposures that are in excess of the amount of investable assets. For example, leverage can be used to create an exposure of one and a half dollars for every dollar invested.

Leveraged buyout (LBO). An acquisition in which the acquiring company buys out the target company using borrowed funds, often in a hostile fashion.

Liquidation. The sale of assets for cash, sometimes to pay off debt.

Liquidity. The ability of an investor to sell an asset in a timely fashion. When there are few buyers for a particular asset, that asset is said to be illiquid.

Mark to market. Determining the price one can get today for currently owned securities.

Market. A place where buyers and sellers of securities make exchanges. Historically, markets have been tangible places such as the New York Stock Exchange or the Chicago Board of Options Exchange, but the advent of networked computers has transferred much of the "action" to cyberspace.

Maturity date. The date on which a bond is redeemed (a five-year bond comes to maturity five years after it is issued).

MBS pass-throughs. Securities that allow investors to participate in cash flows produced by pooled mortgage loans made on single-family residences.

Mortgage-backed security (MBS). A security that represents an ownership interest in mortgage loans made by financial institutions such as savings and loans, commercial banks, or mortgage companies, to finance the borrower's purchase of a home.

Net market exposure. The percentage of a portfolio that is exposed to market fluctuations because long positions are not matched by equal dollar amounts of short positions. Roughly:

$$\text{Market exposure} = \frac{(\text{Long exposure} - \text{Short exposure})}{\text{Capital}}.$$

Option-adjusted spread (OAS). The average spread over the Treasury yield curve that equates a mortgage-backed security's observed market price with an estimated present value of future MBS cash flows. The OAS can be interpreted as the security's incremental return over Treasuries, adjusted for the effects of interest-rate volatility and its impact on the MBS's prepayment tendencies.

Par value. The face value of a bond, or the amount it is redeemed for at maturity.

Planned amortization class (PAC) bonds. Collateralized mortgage obligations (CMOs) broken down into classes with differing average lives that use support bonds to offer a fixed principal schedule that will hold over a range of prepayment scenarios.

Position.   A particular holding within a portfolio (for example, 1,000 shares of Citigroup).

Prepayment duration.   The price sensitivity of mortgage-backed securities to moves in prepayment rates, independent of other variables.

Prepayments.   Mortgage payments that a borrower makes before they are due.

Pure arbitrage.   The simultaneous purchase and sale of the same instruments at different prices when the risk to profit is zero. For example, if you buy gold for $100 on one side of the street, walk across the street, and sell it for $110 on the other side, you are making a 10 percent "sure" profit on the simultaneous buy and sell.

Qualitative analysis.   Assessment of those factors that cannot be quantified yet are integral to the future success of the company.

Quantitative fundamental analysis.   The examination of quantifiable statistical indications of a company's financial well-being.

Relative value arbitrage.   The simultaneous purchase and sale of related instruments, wherein the profit on such a trade depends on a favorable change in the relationship between the prices of the instruments.

Repurchase agreement or Repo.   The financing of specific bonds long or short.

Sector.   A group of companies that are similar either in what they produce or in their market—for example, healthcare, biotechnology, financial, or Internet. A segment of the economy can also be a sector.

Sequential-pay CMOs.   Collateralized mortgage obligations (CMOs) broken down into classes with differing average lives.

Short interest rebate.   The interest earned on the cash proceeds of a short sale of stock.

Short selling.   Borrowing a security and selling it on the open market, and buying it back later (ideally, at a lower price). The intention is to benefit from a decrease in the price of the security. Short positions can be taken as hedges for an associated long position, or as stand-alone investments.

Speculator.   An investor who makes large directional bets on what financial markets will do next.

Spread.   The difference between the prices of two comparable or related securities. A spread is measured in basis points. One basis point equals 1/100 of

1 percent. For example, because corporate bonds of comparable maturity and comparable coupon rates will have higher yields than Treasuries of similar maturity, to reflect their greater default risk, their yields are often quoted as a spread above the Treasury rate. The riskier the bond issue, the larger the spread.

Static return.   Returns such as interest income from coupon payments and short interest rebates from short sales of stock that are unaffected by price fluctuations of the underlying securities.

Stock selection risk.   Exposure to uncertainty about the future valuation of a particular stock.

Stock swap merger.   A merger in which the holders of the target company's stock receive shares of the acquiring company's stock rather than cash.

Strategic acquisition.   A noncompetitive acquisition in which the acquiring company has a good business reason for the merger, such as expanding product capability.

Systemic risk factors.   Factors, such as interest rates or the price of oil, that have the ability to systematically affect the valuation of a whole range of stocks if they change.

TED spreads.   Originally, spreads of Treasuries over Eurodollars; now, all global government bonds hedged against par swaps in the same currency.

Time horizon analysis.   Examination of the time frame for completion of a corporate event.

Trading positions.   Opportunistic positions designed to take advantage of short-term market mispricings and inefficiencies.

Value investing.   Buying out-of-favor securities that are priced cheaply, and holding them until they return to favor.

Yield.   The single investment rate that sets the present value of all of a bond's future cash payments equal to the price of the bond.

Yield curve arbitrage.   Fixed-income trades that involve taking long and short positions at different points on the U.S. Treasury yield curve, to profit from relative pricing disparities.

Index

About Bloomberg

> For in-depth market information and news, visit Bloomberg.com, which draws proprietary content from the BLOOMBERG PROFESSIONAL™ service and Bloomberg's host of media products to provide high-quality news and information in multiple languages on stocks, bonds, currencies, and commodities—at **www.bloomberg.com.**

Bloomberg LP, founded in 1981, is a global information services, news, and media company. Headquartered in New York, the company has nine sales offices, two data centers, and 80 news bureaus worldwide.

Bloomberg Financial Markets, serving customers in 100 countries around the world, holds a unique position within the financial services industry by providing an unparalleled combination of news, information, and analytic tools in a single package known as the BLOOMBERG PROFESSIONAL™ service. Corporations, banks, money management firms, financial exchanges, insurance companies, and many other entities and organizations rely on Bloomberg as their primary source of information.

BLOOMBERG NEWS[SM], founded in 1990, offers worldwide coverage of economies, companies, industries, governments, financial markets, politics, and sports. The news service is the main content provider for Bloomberg's broadcast media, which include BLOOMBERG TELEVISION®—the 24-hour cable and satellite television network available in ten languages worldwide—and BLOOMBERG RADIO™—an international radio network anchored by flagship station BLOOMBERG® RADIO AM 1130 in New York.

In addition to the BLOOMBERG PRESS® line of books, Bloomberg publishes BLOOMBERG® Magazine, BLOOMBERG PERSONAL FINANCE™, and BLOOMBERG® WEALTH MANAGER. To learn more about Bloomberg, call a sales representative at:

Frankfurt:	49-69-920-410	San Francisco:	1-415-912-2960
Hong Kong:	852-977-6000	São Paulo:	5511-3048-4500
London:	44-171-330-7500	Singapore:	65-438-8585
New York:	1-212-318-2000	Sydney:	61-29-777-8686
Princeton:	1-609-279-3000	Tokyo:	81-3-3201-8900

About the Author

Joseph G. Nicholas is a leading authority on hedge funds and alternative investment strategies. Mr. Nicholas is Founder and Chairman of Hedge Fund Research LLC (HFR), an SEC registered investment adviser specializing in structuring and managing fund of funds and multiple manager portfolios, and Hedge Fund Research, Inc., a leading supplier of data on hedge funds, including the HFR Databases, the industry's largest and most comprehensive hedge fund databases. Mr. Nicholas also cofounded the Zurich HFR Index Funds, the first strategy pure, daily priced, fully transparent, investable market-neutral and hedge fund strategy indices. Mr. Nicholas is author of *Investing In Hedge Funds: Strategies for the New Marketplace (Bloomberg Press)*, is a frequent lecturer on topics relating to alternative investments, and has appeared on CNN and Nightly Business Report. Mr. Nicholas received a Bachelor of Science Degree in Commerce from DePaul University and the degree of Juris Doctor from Northwestern University School of Law.